The Open University

Arts: A Second Level Course
Seventeenth-century England: A Changing Culture, 1618–1689

The Sixteen-Fifties

Prepared for the course team by Trevor Bray, Christopher Hill and Anne Laurence

The Open University Press

Cover illustrations

Front The Commonwealth ruling with a standing army. (Ashmolean Museum, Oxford.)

Back James Nayler being punished for his blasphemy. (Engraving by unknown artist for Ephraim Pagit, *Heresiography: or a description of the heretickes of these latter times*, 5th edition, 1654. (Mansell Collection.)

The Open University Press
Walton Hall, Milton Keynes
MK7 6AA

First published 1981. Reprinted 1984.

Designed by the Graphic Design Group of the Open University.

Printed in Great Britain by
Eyre & Spottiswoode Limited at Grosvenor Press, Portsmouth.

ISBN 0 335 11040 1

This text forms part of an Open University course. The complete list of the course appears at the end of this text.

For general availability of supporting material referred to in this text, please write to Open University Educational Enterprises Limited, 12 Cofferidge Close, Stony Stratford, Milton Keynes, MK11 1BY, Great Britain.

Further information on Open University courses may be obtained from the Admissions Office, The Open University, PO Box 48, Walton Hall, Milton Keynes, MK7 6AB.

1.2

Block 6　The Sixteen-Fifties

Contents

Introduction to Block 6

The subject of this block is the sixteen-fifties. In the first part Christopher Hill examines the period as one of consolidation following the turmoil of the sixteen-forties. Anne Laurence then discusses one of the most unpopular attempts by Cromwell to solve the problems of finding a form of government which would satisfy both the gentry and the army.

The next four parts all look at different responses to Puritanism. In 'The State Church' we look at the attempts to find a religious settlement which would satisfy those who wanted a state church and those who wanted religious toleration. You can listen to the debate on toleration in the trial of the Quaker James Nayler (on Cassette 4). In 'Millenarianism and Fifth Monarchism' and 'The Breakdown of Calvinism' we look at the ideas which challenged both the religious and the political premises of Puritanism. You can listen to George Fox's views on the corruption of the established church on Cassette 3.

In the last two parts we look at the impression that Puritanism made upon scientific thinking and intellectual innovation and upon music. There is also a radio programme on music and the Commonwealth, Radio programme 8, *Puritans and Church Music*. Radio 9, *Milton and his Times*, and TV 9, *Marvell: 'Upon Appleton House'*, show us how two great literary figures respond to the sixteen-fifties and look forward to Block 7, *Milton and Marvell*, in which their work is studied in more detail.

Set books

You will need the following set books as you work through Block 6.

Christopher Hill (revised edition 1980) *The Century of Revolution*, Nelson (referred to as *C of R*).
Ann Hughes (ed.) (1980) *Seventeenth Century England: A Changing Culture*, Volume 1, *Primary Sources*, Ward Lock (referred to as the Anthology).
W. R. Owens (ed.) (1980) *Seventeenth Century England: A Changing Culture*, Volume 2, *Modern Studies*, Ward Lock (referred to as the Reader).
Helen Gardner (ed.) (1957) *The Metaphysical*, Penguin.

You will also need the cassette notes which accompany Cassettes 3 and 4.

Cassettes and record

Cassette 3 (AC207) and Cassette 4 (AC208).

Record 1, *Seventeenth-century England: Music 1* (OU69).

The Sixteen-Fifties: Decade of Consolidation

(Before you start you should read or reread *C of R*, pages 97–100, 113–18, 137–8, 147–9.)

Most historians would agree that the sixteen-fifties saw an ebbing of the revolutionary tide. They would disagree on dating the high point. Was it in 1647 when Agitators nearly captured the army, in 1649 with the execution of Charles I, proclamation of the republic and defeat of the Levellers, or in 1653 with the Barebones Parliament? In that year the Rump of the Long Parliament had been dissolved by a coalition in which, for the last time, radicals and conservatives in the army united. But the Barebones Parliament proved impotent because it represented both wings: only with its self-dissolution in December 1653 did the conservatives triumph.

With the setting up of the Protectorate of Oliver Cromwell in December 1653 a period of consolidation and conservatism is evident. Radicals in the army were purged. The Instrument of Government witnessed a return to a Parliament elected by the propertied classes, albeit on a redistributed franchise. The gentry slowly returned to dominate local government, taking over from the rather lower social classes who had run the county committees with army support from the time of the Civil War (see 'The Civil War and the Provinces' in Block 4). There was a brief interlude of renewed army rule under the Major-Generals, but this was repudiated in the Parliament of 1656, and the Petition and Advice established something recognizably like the old constitution, with two chambers and a Protector empowered to nominate his successor. King Charles II proved to be in many ways the heir to Protector Oliver.

We can illustrate this growing conservatism in many ways. In March 1649 the Leveller leaders were arrested, and mutinies in the army suppressed. In May there were more serious mutinies in regiments scheduled to go to Ireland, but these were decisively defeated at Burford. That was the end of the Leveller movement. Lilburne died in gaol, a Quaker, in 1657. Levellers like Overton, Wildman and Sexby compromised themselves by conspiring with Royalists and Spaniards against the Protectorate – a measure of their political despair. In the summer of 1650 the Digger colonies were suppressed, and that was the end of the Digger movement. In August 1650 the Blasphemy Act was aimed especially against the Ranters, and in 1651 leading figures like Coppe and Clarkson escaped severe penalties only by public recantation; and that was the end of the Ranters, though some of them passed into the Quaker movement. If you listen to the debates on the Nayler case on Cassette 4, you will realize how worried MPs were about radical aspects of the Quaker movement in 1656. The savage punishment inflicted on James Nayler was their reaction.

How did conservative consolidation work out in practice? It was a drift, a mood, rather than a consistently pursued policy. The essential first step was for the government of the Commonwealth to re-establish relations with the City of London and the Parliamentarian gentry, relations which had been shattered by the army's coup against Parliament in 1647, by Pride's Purge in December 1648 and the execution of the King in January 1649. From the Rump's earliest days efforts were made to persuade MPs excluded in December 1648 to return to the House. The government's suppression of the Levellers won warm City approval – as well as praise from the Presbyterian Ralph Josselin. The conquest of Ireland was also popular in the City, many of whose merchants had advanced money for this purpose in the early forties. They now got their return in Irish land. Officers and soldiers of the New Model Army too shared in the plunder of Ireland, often receiving claims on confiscated land in lieu of arrears of wages. Few rank-and-file soldiers seem to have settled there: they sold their claims to speculators, and many of the new owners of Irish land were absentee English monied men.

As we saw in Block 4, the Navigation Act of 1651 put into effect a policy which merchants had been calling for since at least the sixteen-twenties. The naval power of the Commonwealth was far greater than that of the monarchy had ever been, and this power was now put behind an aggressive foreign policy designed to achieve economic ends. The Navigation Act challenged the Dutch to fight for the carrying trade of the world. They took up the challenge and were defeated in the first Dutch War of 1652–4. Blake's fleet in the Mediterranean from 1654 onwards gave the protection to English merchants there that James and Charles had never been able to provide, and so powerfully reinforced England's export drive. Cromwell's Western Design of 1655, although not fully successful, satisfied the aspirations of another trading group by conquering Jamaica and so establishing a base for the slave trade in the western hemisphere. The conquest of Dunkirk in 1658 cleaned up a piratical stronghold which had long troubled English traders, and consolidated English control of the Channel. In 1656 the Merchant Adventurers were confirmed in their privileges, in 1657 the East India Company received a new charter (see C of R, page 132). So in all respects the governments of the fifties attempted to restore good relations with the City. Cromwell's anti-Spanish foreign policy, as I suggested in Block 4, may have helped to reconcile some Royalists to the Protectorate.

The year 1647 had also seen a breach between the army and the gentry, many of whom withdrew or were excluded from local government. Slowly they were persuaded and cajoled back. But this was a longer and more difficult process than recovering the City's confidence. One constant fact in the seventeenth century was that any House of Commons representative of 'the natural rulers' would be opposed to the existence of a standing army and indeed to any central power strong enough to interfere with their control of local government, whether it was the power of Laud, or of the Major-Generals, or of James II. The gentry traditionally officered the militia, and they wanted this to be the only armed force in the country. A second constant fact was that any 'freely elected' House of Commons would oppose religious toleration. The constitutions of the sixteen-fifties were attempts to bridge this gap between the government and the 'natural rulers'.

EXERCISE

Please read extracts 98–100 in the Anthology – Cromwell's speeches. How would you summarize the difference in his attitude to the two Parliaments?

DISCUSSION

In 1653 Cromwell was full of optimistic and utopian enthusiasm; by 1654 he was a sadder and more disillusioned man. In this more conservative mood he set out on the path of reconciliation with 'the natural rulers'.

The Instrument of Government was produced by a group around Major-General Lambert in December 1653, after the dissolution of the Barebones Parliament. It set up an elective Lord Protector (Oliver Cromwell), and placed legislative authority firmly in the hands of a triennial Parliament. The Protector could delay legislation for twenty days but had no veto. Great officers of state were to be chosen 'by the approbation of Parliament'. The franchise was redistributed, with a significant shift from boroughs to counties. Seats in Parliament were given to Scotland and Ireland, recently united with England. Perhaps the most important point of the constitution was its nomination of a Council of fifteen members who had very great powers and were virtually irremovable except by death. This Council enshrined the power of the generals. Payment of the army was written into the constitution. A very broad non-compulsive state church was confirmed, with toleration for Protestants outside it. Tithes were to continue until some better way of paying the clergy was devised.

As soon as Oliver's first Parliament met it attacked this constitution.

The Proposed Parliamentary Constitution, its alternative, would have sub-ordinated executive, judges, army, militia and foreign policy to Parliament. The sums to be raised in taxation for the army would have been drastically reduced. The Council would have lost its key position. Election of the Protector's successor would have been removed from Council to Parliament. The Protector would have been given the right to confer hereditary titles *with Parliament's consent*. The old franchise would have been restored, but the redistribution of seats was to be accepted. Religious toleration would have been seriously curtailed. Tithes were to be maintained. Parliament was dissolved without this constitution becoming law.

Cromwell's second Parliament met in 1656–7 and tried again to revise the constitution. In between had come first the rule of the Major-Generals, which intensified the desire of the 'natural rulers' for a civil solution (see Anne Laurence, pages 10–18) and then Nayler's symbolic entry into Bristol, which intensified their hatred of the religious toleration favoured by the Protector and the army, and still guaranteed by the Instrument of Government. (For the Nayler case, see below pages 26–7.) The Humble Petition and Advice offered the crown to Oliver Cromwell, and provided for the creation of a second chamber. Duly elected MPs were not to be excluded (as they had been in 1654 and 1656); in future all disputed elections would be tried by Commissioners appointed by Act of Parliament. Councillors were to be approved by Parliament, and not removed without its consent. A larger revenue was voted than in the Proposed Parliamentary Constitution, but the clause 'no part thereof to be raised by a land tax' and provision for complete Parliamentary control of taxation more than compensated. Religious toleration was further restricted: 'blasphemers' and disturbers of public worship (like Quakers) were to be punished. When Oliver refused the offer of the crown, but accepted the rest of the constitution, he was given the right to nominate his successor as Lord Protector.

EXERCISE

Can you arrive at any general conclusions about the objectives of these written constitutions? Why did they feature at this period of English history and in no other?

DISCUSSION

1   Compare what was said about the Heads of the Proposals in 'Ideas about the State', Block 5. The constitutions were the product of specific political situations, not of arm-chair philosophizing. A main object of the Instrument of Government was to prevent power wholly returning to the 'natural rulers' – by writing the power of the generals into the constitution and guaranteeing finance for the army. Its extension of the electorate also aimed to reduce the influence of landlords, as well as to give better representation to areas of growing economic importance. The Proposed Parliamentary Constitution and the Petition and Advice each signified a move away from Army power, emphasizing 'the law of the land', the sovereignty of Parliaments, and especially Parliamentary control over taxation (and consequently over the army) and the power of the 'natural rulers' in local affairs. But when the army collapsed in 1659–60 the Petition and Advice lost its significance. It had been an anti-constitution.

2   The end of prerogative courts, bishops and the traditional Privy Council left a weakened executive after the Civil War. But the army takeover in December 1648 changed all that. The House of Lords, although certainly no less important politically than the House of Commons, had on occasion mediated between government and Commons – e.g. over the Petition of Right. Its abolition together with the monarchy left no constitutional check on an executive directly dependent on the House of Commons. The 'natural rulers' disliked a powerful executive. In 1657 the Petition and Advice forced the generals to step down from the Council, but they were still powerful

enough to insist on strong representation in the Other House, which became something very different from a House of Lords. After the collapse of the Protectorate in April 1659 the shibboleth of the generals became 'a select senate' – an upper chamber with a veto, composed of course of themselves, their friends and relations.

Reconciling the gentry to army rule looks like trying to square the circle – something which even Thomas Hobbes failed to do. But this is perhaps the result of our hindsight. We know that Oliver Cromwell was to die in 1658, and that his son and successor Richard failed to keep the army united. But if Oliver had lived as long as Queen Elizabeth – another ten years – the history of England might have been very different. He always had his sights fixed on a 'settlement'.

In 1659–60 radicalism revived, and the consequent social panic drove former Parliamentarians and former Royalists into one another's arms. The peaceful restoration of Charles II was the result (see Block 8, *The Restoration*). But so long as the army remained united it could never have been overthrown by either Royalist or radical revolt; attempts in 1649, 1651, 1655, 1657 and even 1659 were all totally unsuccessful. The decade saw greater prosperity than England had known for a long time. Some men were getting rich quickly. Many gentlemen were in process of successfully reorganizing agricultural production after absorbing land purchases and adjusting both to the abolition of feudal tenures and to the new levels of taxation (see Block 4, 'Economic and Foreign Policy, 1642–60'). What most of the propertied class seem to have wanted above all was a return to 'normality' – reduced taxes, an end to military arbitrariness, restoration of the rule of law. In 1660 the only way to get this seemed to be by restoring Charles II. But things had looked different earlier.

Consider some of the literary evidence. Marvell's 'An Horatian Ode upon Cromwell's Return from Ireland' (*The Metaphysical Poets*, page 258), which presumably dates from 1650, accepts the fact of the Revolution, despite the poet's personal sympathy for Charles I. It looks forward to an epoch of foreign conquest under Cromwell's rule. In 1651 Thomas Hobbes, who had fled from England in 1640, published *Leviathan* and returned to England. He claimed that this work persuaded many Royalists to accept the Commonwealth – as he had done. The intellectual eminence of *Leviathan* should not make us forget that it was only one of several tracts published in the years 1649–51 – by John Dury, Francis Rous, Anthony Ascham, Marchamont Nedham – all advocating acceptance of the Commonwealth government because it was the effective ruler of the country and therefore should be supported even by those who had hitherto opposed it out of loyalty to the monarchy. They called for a pragmatic approach to politics, an 'end of ideology'. (Quentin Skinner discusses these writers in Radio Programme 7, *Hobbes*). Hobbes's barbs were directed equally against advocates of the Divine Right of Kings and radical enthusiasts.

There are many signs that a mood of exhaustion led to revulsion from divisive ideological politics. The year 1651 had seen the final rout of Scots and Royalists at the Battle of Worcester. The complete subjugation of Scotland to England followed that of Ireland. The same year saw Milton's *Defence of the People of England*, attempting to reunite his countrymen on patriotic grounds; it also saw Gerrard Winstanley's dedication to Oliver Cromwell of *The Law of Freedom* ('you have power . . ., I have no power'). Former Royalists like Sir William Davenant, Abraham Cowley and Walter Charleton began to show signs of wishing to come to terms, ideologically as well as politically, with their victorious enemies. In 1657 the Duke of Buckingham, England's only non-royal Duke, followed Hobbes's example and returned to England, marrying Fairfax's daughter (the heroine of Marvell's 'Upon Appleton House'). Given time, who knows how many might have followed him? Cromwell's aggressive foreign policy certainly appealed to traditional patriotic sentiment. Charles I's poet laureate, Davenant, wrote anti-Spanish operas for presentation at Cromwell's increasingly regal court.

Interesting in this respect are the attempts to reinvigorate a broad state church. From the sixteen-forties the army had defended religious toleration. Many radicals thought, like Milton, that the abolition of a state church was essential to religious liberty. They came to see tithes as the crucial issue. So did conservatives who wished to preserve a state church. Attitudes towards tithes are an index of political attitudes: this is argued below in 'The State Church, 1640–60'.

The 'free Parliament' of 1660 restored gentry control – with the approval of the City of London – under a new consensus which replaced that of the Tudor age, though this time the uniting factor was fear of social radicalism. No written constitution was imposed, because the emphasis was on returning to tradition, to normality: there seemed in 1660 no need to protect 'the natural rulers' against the executive. That problem arose only later (see 'From the Restoration to 1688' in Block 8, *The Restoration*). From the point of view of conservatives, a main advantage of the restoration of monarchy in 1660 was that it closed the door on constitutional discussions. Ireton in the Putney Debates had pointed out that it was dangerous to try to impose a constitution derived from natural rights. Men, he argued, might disagree endlessly about what natural rights were: one man's natural right was another man's anarchy or communism. In Hobbes's theory of sovereignty, law was the command of the sovereign. It might be arbitrary, but there was no arguing against it. After the upheavals of the Revolution this theory had many attractions for those who had felt that property and social subordination were in danger. So had 'a King with plenty of holy oil about him'.

The Rule of the Major-Generals, 1655–7

Crucial dates

Sept. 1654–Jan. 1655	First Protectorate Parliament.
Nov. 1654–June 1655	Cony's Case.
March 1655	Penruddock's Rising. An abortive rising of Royalists in the west. The other risings planned to take place simultaneously failed to occur.
April 1655	Government proposed to reduce soldiers' pay and to continue the reduction of the army started in 1653
August 1655	First Instructions to the Major-Generals by the Council of State, raising a voluntary militia to secure the country against Royalist plots in the face of a reduced standing army. The militia was to be administered in eleven districts covering England and Wales, over each of which was a Major-General placed in command. The militia was to be maintained by a decimation tax on the royalists.
	Instructions requiring Major-Generals to report on the Ordinance for the ejection of scandalous ministers.
September 1655	Orders for securing the peace of the commonwealth to be executed by government-appointed commissioners for each country under the supervision of the major-generals. The commissioners' primary task was to assess and levy the decimation tax on royalists.
October 1655	Additional Instructions to Major-Generals largely compiled by Lambert.
December 1656	Nayler's trial.
	Major-General Disbrowe brought in a bill to continue the decimation tax on Royalists for the maintenance of the militia.
January 1657	Bill for continuation of decimation read for the first time. Parliament resolved not to give it a second reading, thus ending the rule of the Major-Generals.
March 1660	Militia Bill – authority of gentry in the militia reasserted.
July 1661	Militia Act – sole command of militia in King.

The Rule of The Major-Generals, 1655–7

(Before starting you should read or reread *C of R*, pages 97–8 and 114–17. You should also remind yourself of the ideas presented in Christopher Hill's 'The Origins of the Civil War' in Block 3 and Ann Hughes's 'The Civil War and the Provinces' in Block 4.)

Apart from the general theme of court and country, you know that there is a more specific debate amongst historians about the importance of provincial loyalty in the Civil War. We cannot assess how far individuals in the seventeenth century perceived themselves as part of a national community, or as part of a number of smaller communities defined by geography, class, religion or any of a variety of other factors. The debate between historians as to the significance of provincial issues in determining allegiances in the Civil War is just one aspect of this. Christopher Hill suggests in Block 3 that it was fear of social explosion, not loyalty to the county community, or to King or to Parliament which united the gentry and brought them into the war. In Block 4 Anne Hughes suggests that there were complex patterns of regional diversity, but that local studies tend to underestimate profound social changes and deep ideological divisions.

My own view is that whilst county connections were very important to the gentry, the gentry also had a two-way communication with the government at Whitehall and with the Parliament at Westminster. As JPs on the bench and as deputy lieutenants they were appointed by the Crown to implement policy made at Whitehall and Acts of Parliament passed at Westminster, though often interpreting these in their own best interest. As MPs they went to Westminster and participated in national affairs, though often representing local or sectional interests in Parliament. So the gentry represented local interests in a national forum and national interests in their localities. What they resented was any attempt to cut off this two-way communication. When Parliament wasn't sitting they resorted to the law courts. They did this during the sixteen-thirties and again in the sixteen-fifties. In 1654 George Cony, a merchant, refused to pay duty on imported silk. This was more an attempt to register a protest at the impotence of Parliament than at Cromwell's failure to call it. But it also represented an outright challenge to the Instrument of Government.

I want now to look at the period between March 1655 and January 1657 when there was what the gentry saw as a concerted attempt to undermine the two-way communication between the localities and the centre. In March 1655 there took place the abortive Royalist Western rising, often called after one of its leaders, John Penruddock. It was to have been accompanied by simultaneous risings in other parts of the country, but these failed to materialize. After the rising Royalists were arrested and imprisoned without warrant. The government found itself with a grave problem of security. It needed a form of local administration which would combat Royalist conspiracy and maintain vigilance over dissident activity. But it was already unable to pay what remained of the standing army, let alone any extra forces.

As a result of these problems, a new expedient was devised. A militia was to be formed of volunteers. The soldiers, mainly cavalry, were to be paid constantly, but called out only in emergencies. Clarendon suggested that Cromwell's intention was to create a force strong enough to control the standing army should it get out of control, although there is little evidence to support this theory. The standing army was to be further reduced and the militia was to be financed by a new tax. This tax was to be levied on any Royalist, active or passive, whose estate was worth more than £100 a year, and was to amount to a tenth of its value.

To organize the militia and assess and raise the decimation, the country was divided into precincts in charge of which were placed senior army officers, Major-Generals, who were to appoint their own local

11

commissioners to administer the tax. The first Instructions to the Major-Generals in August 1655 created eleven precincts and confined their activities to the decimation and the militia. Further Instructions in September and October added two more precincts, extended the Major-Generals' powers for the maintenance of security, and gave them powers over scandalous clergy, schoolmasters and alehouses.

The intention of the Instructions was 'to preserve the nation from the designs of restless and unwearied enemies', by means of suppressing 'tumults and rebellion'. The Major-Generals were to secure the arms of papists and Royalists, make the highways safe from robberies and burglaries, keep an eye on the disaffected and suppress all meetings (including cock-fighting, horse racing and bear-baiting), enquire after idlers and prevent anyone who had been ejected from a benefice, college or school for delinquency or scandal from keeping school, preaching, or administering the sacraments. They were also to ensure that alehouses were licensed and to keep a check on plays and gaming houses. All that this really amounted to was to ensure that local officials put existing legislation into effect. But, in the first set of Instructions, they were also asked 'to promote godliness and discourage profanity, acting with justices of peace and ministers against drunkenness, blasphemy etc and *to certify justices who are remiss, that they may be dismissed*' (my italics). This implies not just the improvement of existing local government but the imposition by the central government of new coercive powers over local administration. This clause seems to have been left out of the final version of the Instructions (J. P. Kenyon, *Stuart Constitution*, page 349). But the two intentions remained. The Major-Generals exercised a supervisory function over JPs and over morals 'that the laws against drunkenness, blaspheming and taking of the name of God in vain, by swearing and cursing, plays and interludes, and profaning the Lord's Day, and such like wickedness and abominations, be put into more effectual execution than they have been hitherto'.

Figure 1   Major-General John Lambert (1619–84). (National Portrait Gallery.)

The Major-Generals, then, had three main areas of concern: the militia, improving local government, and the general supervision of clergy and morals. In one sense or another each of these was an aspect of security. I want now to look at these areas of activity. The militia was formed as a result of the fear of further Royalist insurrections. Its membership was voluntary. It differed from previous peacetime militias, however, in that its leadership came not from the lieutenancy made up of the local gentry, but rather from the Major-Generals acting directly on instructions from Whitehall. The gentry did not regain control of the militia until the eve of the Restoration.

The organization of the militia shaded into the improvement of local government because of the administration of the decimation, needed to support the militia. Better local government meant efficient tax collection and efficient law enforcement. In particular this involved vigilance over Royalists and other dissidents, preventing them from meeting, and from expressing their views in print or by word of mouth. The Major-Generals appointed commissioners to assess and levy the decimation. They appointed a considerable number of people as commissioners but it is probable that nothing like all of them served. This had also been true of the county committees set up in the early years of the war. To serve as a decimation commissioner implied support of the regime and it is notable that few of the leading gentry were prepared to commit themselves to it.

These commissioners were solely concerned with the administration of the decimation. The Major-Generals also worked with JPs and municipal corporations. Some of the county committees continued to administer the assessment but their role in local government was reduced. The Major-Generals had themselves appointed to the commissions of the peace and, following their instructions from Whitehall, tried to make sure that local magistrates carried out their duties more effectively. Different Major-Generals interpreted this in different ways. Previous governments had tried to supervise local magistrates more closely and to interfere in municipal and parliamentary elections. The Major-Generals' supervision was seen as another attempt at control of the localities from Whitehall. Charles I's attempt to direct JPs had been much resented (*C of R*, pages 24 and 60–1) and the county committees set up in 1643 were seen as unwelcome interference from the centre. The Major-Generals were unpopular because they were the agents of Whitehall and they were effectively intervening in local affairs. But they were not just civil servants. They were members of the army, they were, by and large, strangers to the areas they administered, and they were bypassing the county gentry who expected to run local government.

During the sixteen-fifties various attempts were made to solve the problems resulting from the lack of any ecclesiastical organization, for the Presbyterian system proposed by the Westminster Assembly and legislated by the Long Parliament was only partially implemented. The chief practical problems were those resulting from there being no means of appointing new clergy or getting rid of deficient ones. To this end two commissions were set up in 1654: one for examining suitable candidates and appointing them to vacant benefices (Triers) and one for ejecting unsuitable clergy, whether for their religious or political views or for bad behaviour (Ejectors). The Major-Generals were given the task of seeking out recalcitrant clergy and schoolmasters and passing on their names to the Ejectors. This was another aspect of security, for it was felt that clergy unsympathetic to the regime for religious or political reasons would be bound to influence others to resistance. There was, too, a genuine concern for improving the standards of the clergy and of morals in general. Hence the Major-Generals were to enforce all the laws against vice, against drunkenness, blasphemy, against playhouses, race meetings, gaming houses, 'houses of evil fame', and alehouses. And they were to enforce the proper observation of the Sabbath. It must be said, however, that race meetings, cock-fights and other such gatherings were forbidden not just because they led people into evil ways but because they were identified as occasions when Royalists and other enemies of the regime met and plotted.

One of the most important figures acting behind the scenes in the sixteen-fifties was John Thurloe. Apart from developing a national postal service, he was also in charge of Cromwell's intelligence service. He had worked with Cromwell since 1651, although he was not appointed as secretary to the Council of State until 1652, and continued to serve the Protectorate until 1659. The letters of intelligence which he received and sent out, published in the *Thurloe State Papers*, are one of the major historical sources for the sixteen-fifties. You can see from the letters printed in the Anthology (extracts 101–4) that Thurloe concerned himself not just with security, but with all areas of central and local administration. He maintained a constant correspondence not only with people in different parts of England, but also with Monck in Scotland, with Fleetwood and Henry Cromwell in Ireland, and with agents in Europe, America, and the West Indies.

The *Thurloe State Papers* contain a great deal of information concerning the everyday business of the Major-Generals. The earliest letter dates from October 31st 1655 and is from Major-General Whalley. Whalley corresponded with Thurloe perhaps more than any of the other Major-Generals, although most wrote to him fairly frequently. The amount of the Major-Generals' correspondence with Thurloe increased in the period leading up to the elections to the second Protectorate Parliament in August 1656. Thereafter it declined rapidly, and there is hardly any after September 1656. By contrast, Thurloe continued to write to Monck and to Henry Cromwell.

EXERCISE

Read the letters from the Major-Generals reprinted in the Anthology (extracts 101–4). How far do the Major-Generals seem to be carrying out the same set of Instructions?

DISCUSSION

All the Major Generals were concerned with the appointment of the commissioners for the decimation and with its assessment and administration. These were clearly larger concerns in the first months of the rule of the Major-Generals than later. The problems arising from the assessment were often mentioned and were sometimes referred to the Protector and Council for advice. Perhaps the most important of them was the inability to raise enough money to pay the militia. The appointment of commissioners, JPs and sheriffs was an important part of their work. So was recruitment to the militia, and to the fleet in maritime counties. All of these places were the harder to fill because of the reluctance of many of the gentry to identify themselves with the Protectorate by holding office, even at the county level, under it.

We also see from the letters a general concern with security. Enemies, or supposed enemies, of the regime caused the Major-Generals much anxiety. Amongst them were mentioned malignants and episcopalians (extract 101), Quakers (extract 102), Fifth Monarchists (extract 104), and 'wandering idle persons' (extract 102). A more generalized concern with disaffection amongst the local population emerged as the elections for the second Protectorate Parliament drew near. This was reflected in a renewed interest in appointing suitable men to key local positions, for ensuring that those already holding positions had no cause for complaint against the regime, and for taking sterner measures against possible enemies.

Each Major-General was very much his own man. You've read letters from four of the thirteen men who served as Major-Generals. You can see their concern for the general policy outlined in their Instructions, but you can also see how differently they ran their different regions. Haynes was worried about the lack of money to pay troops and the difficulty of finding fit persons to appoint to local offices. He writes, too, of the threat posed by the presence of malignants, mainly Royalists, and of the possibility of reforming the composition of the corporation of Norwich by recalling its charter. Worsley was concerned, too, about the presence of delinquents, in this case the former Leveller John Wildman, who was a considerable speculator in the sale of crown lands. Worsley also wanted to improve the administration of the ordinance for ejecting scandalous ministers and schoolmasters. He tried to apprehend 'wandering idle persons' and noted the presence of Quakers in the area. Whalley seemed principally concerned, from this letter, with the overcrowding in the gaols, with clearing the country of rogues, and with instituting a national system of weights and measures. However, he was Cromwell's first cousin and was strongly identified with the Protectorate and probably corresponded directly with Cromwell more than the other Major-Generals. Goffe was concerned with the radical disaffection of Levellers and Fifth Monarchists in his area. Haynes, Goffe and Worsley all write with a sense of God's immediate presence: ' a righteous God in the execution of his judgements', 'a visible hand of God', and 'I hope God will turn it to good'.

These letters suggest that within the uniformity of the Instructions to the Major-Generals there was considerable variation in practice. The Instructions were interpreted differently by different people, but also local circumstances and the individual preoccupations of Major-Generals resulted in a different type of administration from precinct to precinct. Of course the differences are not only due to the different characters and concerns of the individual Major-Generals. They are another expression of the regional diversity which Ann Hughes discussed in Block 4.●

Figure 2 Major-General Charles Worsley (1622–56). (Platt Hall City Galleries, Manchester.)

Another very important source for the rule of the Major-Generals is *Ludlow's Memoirs*, but Blair Worden's recent work has modified our views on Ludlow. It is believed that Ludlow wrote his memoirs some time after the Restoration, when he was in exile as a regicide in Switzerland. It was not known how much the original manuscript was edited for publication in 1698–9, but it was assumed that the editorial additions and deletions did not amount to much. Blair Worden recently discovered part of Ludlow's original manuscript in the Bodleian Library in Oxford, covering the period 1660–77. On the basis of this he concludes that much of the original published version of the *Memoirs* was a radically altered and abridged version of what Ludlow actually wrote. Unfortunately, we do not have the original manuscript for the period 1640–60. It is, of course, possible that this part was less heavily edited than the later part, but since the original publication of the *Memoirs* was a part of the controversy about whether there should be a standing army, this is unlikely. Amongst Blair Worden's conclusions we should note that Ludlow appears to have been much more of a religious radical than the published *Memoirs* would suggest, and that he interpreted political events in the light of his millenarian beliefs.

EXERCISE

Read the extracts from *Ludlow's Memoirs* in the Anthology (extract 105). What was Ludlow's view of the Major-Generals?

DISCUSSION

Ludlow considered that the Major-Generals were acting as agents of the army, in whose hands lay ultimate power in the country. He also believed that Cromwell was trying to assume complete control over the army. He considered that the appointment of the Major-Generals was an arbitrary act and that the powers vested in them were unconstitutional. Apart from levying the decimation, he refers to their powers to distrain upon the estates of those who refused to pay the tax. He also objected to their intervention in legal proceedings and in the election of MPs to the second Protectorate Parliament.

Ludlow associated the oppression of the rule of the Major-Generals initially with Cromwell, and not with the Major-Generals themselves. He saw both the decimation and the organization for its assessment and collection as serving Cromwell's self-interest. The liberties of Englishmen were being sacrificed to 'the idol of his own ambition'. For Ludlow the Parliamentarian cause had been betrayed personally by Cromwell. This view contrasts with the commonly held belief that the King's evil counsellors were responsible for the tyranny of the eleven years' personal rule, not the King himself. Even a Puritan like Mrs Hutchinson could write that the King was advised by 'a great rascally company of flatterers and projectors, there were all the corrupted, tottering bishops, and others of the proud, profane clergy of the land, who, by their strong endeavours to disaffect the prince to his honest, godly subjects, and to get of power from him, to afflict those who would not submit to their domination'.

However, Ludlow does seem to have held the view that the Major-Generals, many of them close associates of his from the early years of the war, became more oppressive to further their own interests. He suggests that they sought the confirmation of the Instrument of Government by the second Protectorate Parliament in order to legitimize their own authority, and thus to preserve their own power. He thought originally that Cromwell would support them in this attempt to establish themselves as a self-perpetuating oligarchy 'because there appeared now no way so probable to maintain his own power, as by keeping the army firmly united to him. But ambition had corrupted his understanding to that degree, that he made no scruple to sacrifice these men, who, to say no worse, had enlarged their consciences to an extraordinary size in the execution of his orders, to those who in requital of the favour had promised to make him king'.

Ludlow's view was that the rule of the Major-Generals was an oppressive and arbitrary form of military rule. He referred to this 'detestable project' and to the way in which the Major-Generals 'carried things with unheard of insolence in their several precincts, decimating to extremity whom they pleased, and interrupting the proceedings at law upon petitions of those who pretended themselves aggrieved; threatening such as would not yield ready submission to their orders with transportation to Jamaica . . .; and suffering none to escape their persecution, but those that would betray their own party'. He also makes the point that the most vociferous opposition to the Major-Generals was from lawyers and country gentlemen. ●

What then, are we to make of Ludlow's opinions of the Major-Generals? A number of historians have followed Ludlow and have referred to the rule of the Major-Generals in such terms as 'military despotism' and 'military repression'. I prefer Gerald Aylmer's view that 'The caricature view of them as military satraps and kill-joy Puritans purveyed by anglican-royalist propaganda, and accepted by many historians, at least until the 1890s, will not do. Most [Major-Generals] were extremely careful not to act outside due process of law; apart from raising the Decimation tax and mustering the new militia, their duties were all within the scope of existing laws. Yet they were agents of the central government with power over their localities . . . and some of them did activate 'moral' reform, using existing legal powers in a way that had no precedent . . . And their ultimate sanction, like that of the Protectorate as a whole, was the sword, so, propaganda and popular myth apart, the militarist, kill-joy image has some slight plausibility.' (*State's Servants*, pp. 48–9.)

The real opposition to the Major-Generals came from the lawyers and the gentry, both of which groups were strongly represented in Parliament. However the Major-Generals were an extra-Parliamentary expedient and their opponents had no means of expressing their opposition in the press or while no Parliament was sitting.

As you know from Block 4, censorship lapsed for much of the sixteen-forties and the early sixteen-fifties. By the mid sixteen-fifties it had been reinstated and was enforced with some vigour by some of the Major-Generals. Anthology extract 104 shows Major-General Goffe obtaining assurances from Cole of Southampton that he will no longer distribute certain books. Furthermore, there was hardly any material published during the rule of the Major-Generals expressing opposition to them. In December 1655 the majority of controversial works published were either for or against the Quakers, or concerned with the extent of the magistrate's power over matters of religion. William Prynne, a formidable opponent of Cromwell, published a number of works on the subversion of the fundamental laws by arbitrary power, but these turn out to be attempts to prove that he had been illegally imprisoned, thinly disguised as works on liberty.

The lawyers' objection to the Major-Generals was that there was no check upon them, either through the courts or through Parliament. The gentry shared this objection, but also resented the fact that the Major-Generals interfered in areas which they traditionally controlled: the commissions of the peace and the militia. They had already been partially displaced from this control by the county committees which were instructed from Whitehall. In many counties the most active committee members came from the lesser gentry who had not previously been much involved in county government. With the partial eclipse of the county committees in the early sixteen-fifties the upper gentry might have expected to regain control. Instead they found that men whose rise was the result of successful army careers were taking over local government. Three of the Major-Generals were related to Cromwell by blood or marriage (Fleetwood, Whalley and Disbrowe). Hardly any of them came from the upper county gentry. All the Major-Generals held, at the time of their appointments, senior rank in the army, but most also held senior civilian appointments in the government. Rather than seeing them as part of a military machine, I think that it makes sense to see them as part of a meritocracy which was created by the army.

The army was the means by which men of ability, but lacking family connections, could rise to participate in national affairs. They seem to have been more hampered by not being natives of the areas they administered than by social differences from the local gentry. There must have been some resentment that men from small beginnings should find their way into favour at Whitehall to the extent that they were transplanted to the localities as agents of the central government. This must have seemed a betrayal of trust to local administrators.

The rule of the Major-Generals collapsed in January 1657 when the second Protectorate Parliament was asked to vote to continue the decimation for an unspecified period and voted against it by 124 to 88 votes. Westminster defeated the attempt of Whitehall to dominate the localities and Cromwell was forced to look for another solution to the problem of finding a form of government to which both the gentry and the army would consent.

What, then, did the rule of the Major-Generals achieve? In the short term it achieved a tightening up of certain areas of local administration, but these areas varied according to the interests of the individual Major-Generals. It resulted in the uniting of the moderate and extreme Royalists by the indiscriminate application of the decimation. But there was, through the policing activities of the Major-Generals, an almost complete cessation of Royalist activity in England and Wales. In the medium term it resulted in the alienation of many of the moderate county gentry from the central government, an alienation which was not to be overcome until the Cavalier Parliament. It created an enduring dislike and suspicion of standing armies amongst both radicals and conservatives. Finally, it confirmed the idea that Cromwell was maintaining himself in power through the military.

References

Gerald Aylmer (1978) *The State's Servants*, Routledge and Kegan Paul.

C. H. Firth (ed.) (1894) *The Memoirs of Edmund Ludlow*.

J. P. Kenyon (1966) *Stuart Constitution, 1603–88*, Cambridge University Press.

Edmund Ludlow, *A Voyce from the Watch Tower*, edited and with an introduction by A. B. Worden, Camden Society, 1978.

The State Church, 1640–60

(Start by reading or rereading pages 139–49 of *C of R*, and re-read Anne Laurence on 'The Sects' in Block 4.)

A major problem for us in considering the state church between 1640 and 1660 is that we know the end of the story. We know that after 1660 bishops will be restored, and that there will be organized sects *permanently* outside the Church of England and existing independently of it – Presbyterians, Independents (Congregationalists), Baptists, Quakers, etc. When we come across these names earlier we naturally tend to equate the beliefs of the groups so named with the post-1660 sects. But to do this is wrong. Those whom we call Presbyterians in the forties and fifties regarded themselves as – and indeed were – members of the Church of England. So did many of those whom we call Independents. They argued about how this church should be organized, but they had no intention of leaving it. They did not choose to leave it in 1660-2: they were *excluded*. There were no distinct Presbyterian or Independent sects before 1660. Baptists were beginning to organize themselves separately, but some Baptists were ministers in the state church in the fifties. Only the Quakers were organized on a sectarian basis from the start.

There were therefore no hard and fast lines distinguishing between people to whom we now attach sectarian labels. Bunyan is variously described as a Baptist and an Independent. In the forties and fifties many men passed easily from one congregation to another, without feeling that they had abandoned one '-ism' and committed themselves to a different one. (If you look at the extracts from Thomas Edwards and Laurence Clarkson in the Anthology (extracts 64 and 83), you will find that they both make this point, though in completely different ways.)

It follows from this that we should not think of the period between the collapse of episcopacy in the early sixteen-forties and its restoration in 1660 as a period in which there was no Church of England. It was a period in which this church was under different management. Some organs of the pre-1640 church were indeed abolished, and remained abolished throughout these decades – church courts, visitations, the Court of High Commission. (The latter was not restored in 1660.) The state took over many functions hitherto performed by the church – censorship, for instance. JPs succeeded to many of the supervisory functions of church courts. The latter indeed ceased to enforce conformity and ecclesiastical 'discipline', their most unpopular functions; but they continued for some time after their formal abolition to carry out routine functions in relation to probate of wills, etc.

Laudian episcopacy was succeeded – after an interval of almost non-government in the church – by a Presbyterian-erastian establishment from 1646 to 1648 (with *de facto* toleration of congregations outside it), then by a semi-voluntary Presbyterian establishment (plus religious toleration) after the state ceased to enforce uniformity; from 1654 there was a looser, more oecumenical broad Protestant church, which in its turn lost government support in 1659–60. But throughout this period most ministers continued to hold their livings, despite the changes. This does not mean that a clergyman who before 1640 had conformed to the Laudian establishment became a 'Presbyterian' in the sixteen-forties, an 'Independent' in the fifties, and an 'Anglican' again after 1660. He almost certainly regarded himself as an 'Anglican' throughout the period, a member of the established Church of England. No doubt he had his preferences for Laudianism or Presbyterianism or Independency or something else, but most ministers stayed put throughout the changes and complied as much or as little as they thought right (or safe) with the outward demands of the state church.

This was not necessarily an attitude of insincere men concerned only to retain their 'livings', though no doubt some had no higher motive. But others would feel that their major duty was to look after the spiritual welfare of their parishioners; changes in the management of the Church of England would seem of relatively minor importance compared with this continuing pastoral function. What most ministers – time-servers as well as dedicated pastors – would regard as important was the existence of the state church and of the tithes which maintained its ministers. Sectarian voluntarists like Milton, on the other hand, believed that true religious liberty could exist only if the church was totally disestablished, and all ministers were dependent on the voluntary contributions of their congregations.

This was much the most important dividing issue of the period. An episcopalian could accept an erastian-Presbyterian or a Cromwellian state church as the lesser evil, just as men who would have preferred a Presbyterian or Independent church before 1640 conformed as long as they could. In the late sixteen-forties a number of 'Independent' MPs became elders of the 'Presbyterian' state church. This was neither illogical nor hypocritical: the church as reorganized in 1646 was the best they could hope for at the moment. The fact that they would have preferred further reform was no reason for cutting themselves off from the national church. On the contrary, it was their duty to try from within to steer the church in the direction which they thought right. Only sectaries who on principle totally disapproved of any state church would think of leaving it. Richard Hooker's dictum remained true for all but very radical Englishmen: 'There is not . . . a member of the commonwealth which is not also a member of the Church of England' (quoted in *C of R*, page 63). It came as a very great shock to such men to be driven out of the state church after 1660.

When the Long Parliament met in November 1640, few voices were raised in defence of the Laudian innovations, or indeed of the all-powerful Laudian hierarchy. The House of Commons set up a Grand Committee for Religion in the first weeks of its existence. In April 1641 a bill was passed against Laud's innovations. In December twelve bishops were impeached; two months later bishops were excluded from the House of Lords. Some 'scandalous' ministers were evicted from their livings: pluralists were reduced to one cure apiece. Laud was executed in January 1645. Next year episcopacy was abolished.

An Assembly of Divines was summoned to draw up a new system of church government (the Westminster Assembly). When it first met, in July, 1643, there was still a possibility that some form of limited episcopacy would survive. So long as the Civil War continued, most MPs were anxious to avoid divisive discussions of ecclesiastical organization or theology. But the Scots – allies from September 1643 – were adamant in their opposition to episcopacy. The war moreover had its own logic. The collapse of the repressive organs of the hierarchy, and of the censorship, meant that separatist sectaries came up from underground, met and preached publicly, defended their cause verbally and in print. Since almost all such sectaries were hostile to Laud and to Charles I's personal government, it was no moment for Parliament to forfeit their support by insisting on strict conformity. (Conformity to what, anyway?) So a good deal of 'liberty to tender consciences' established itself in fact if not in theory.

But at once problems arose. Read the extracts from Thomas Edwards and Thomas Hall in the Anthology (extracts 64 and 71). Similar points were made by MPs in the Nayler debates (see Cassette 4). Although the Nayler debates were slightly later, the hysterical and panicky tone of such conservatives accurately reflects the reaction in the early forties to the sort of things sectaries were saying and doing.

What frightened conservatives was the social implication of the very existence of religious toleration. Christopher Hill indicated the reasons for this in *C of R*, pages 142–3, which it might be helpful to re-read. Conservatives were profoundly disturbed by the idea that ordinary people could meet under their own auspices, and elect their own 'mechanic preacher', an artisan like themselves who worked with his hands six days a week. Unsupervised by a clergyman educated at Oxford or Cambridge, or by a local gentleman, such congregations could discuss whatever they liked, not confining themselves – as no preacher did in the seventeenth century – to subjects which we today would regard as 'religious'. Plurality of wives and communism were probably discussed less frequently than men like Thomas Hall suspected; but the possibility existed. Control had slipped.

Cromwell was suspected of favouring sectaries in his Eastern Association army, because their commitment to the cause made them better fighters than gentlemen with no principled involvement. The alliance which brought a Scottish army into England in 1644 was made primarily for military reasons; but some certainly hoped that the army of Presbyterian Scots would counterbalance such radical forces as Cromwell's. One of the conditions on which the Scots insisted, indeed, was that England should bring her church into conformity with the Kirk of Scotland. Scottish commissioners joined the Westminster Assembly. In July 1645 the Assembly presented to Parliament a form of church government which was essentially an adaptation of the Scottish Presbyterian system. A minority of Independent divines in the Assembly dissented, and Parliament insisted on amendments to insure against a new clerical domination. For instance, there was to be a right of appeal from the proposed hierarchy of church courts to a Parliamentary committee. No Presbyterian High Commission, no Scottish General Assembly of the Kirk!

In August 1646 Parliament authorized the creation of a Presbyterian form of church government for England and Wales. In some parts of England parochial presbyteries and classical organizations came into being – we know of active *classes* in London, Lancashire, Nottingham, Wirksworth (Derbyshire), Essex, Shropshire, Durham and Leeds. Provincial assemblies were erected in London and Lancashire, and the London assembly assumed a general advisory role within England, in the absence of a national synod. The system contrasts with that in Scotland in several ways. First, it was far less clerical; there was a right of appeal from church assemblies to Parliament's committee, and there was to be no interference with existing rights of lay patronage. Secondly, after the army's takeover of political power in 1648, the system lost its coercive powers (never very effectively exercised) and became in effect voluntary. Thirdly, many groups of clergy and laity coexisted within the church who were not in any sense committed to Presbyterianism, a number of them in congregations which were virtually autonomous. (Look at extract 66 in your Anthology, 'The Propositions of Newcastle', for the Presbyterian–Parliamentarian attitude.) Meanwhile the political situation was being transformed by the growing influence of the New Model Army. This army had been made possible by the Self-Denying Ordinance, which deprived members of Parliament of their military commands. Socially this was an extremely radical measure, in that it removed all peers from the army: military command had been time out of mind the especial social function of the aristocracy. To add insult to injury, Oliver Cromwell somehow was restored to his command despite his membership of the House of Commons; and with the startling series of victories for the New Model in 1645, ending three years military stale-mate, the influence of dedicated supporters of religious toleration became irresistible.

Many congregations and ministers had long enjoyed considerable latitude of organization and worship, and it was now difficult to bring them into conformity with the 'lame erastian presbytery', as the Scots called the English church. ('Erastian' in this context means 'subordinated to the secular authority'.) Within the Westminster Assembly there had been a vociferous minority of ministers (Thomas Goodwin, Philip Nye, Sidrach Simpson, Jeremiah Burroughs and William Bridge) arguing for a non-Presbyterian form of church organization.

EXERCISE

Look at the section from *An Apologeticall Narration* (extract 63 in your Anthology). What do the five dissenting brethren ask for?

DISCUSSION

They ask for the right of gathered congregations (under orthodox ministers and ruled with the co-operation of lay elders) to be free from control by a clerical hierarchy. Congregations would consult with one another, but there would be no over-riding outside authority except that of the secular power. Not unnaturally, this position had its attraction for MPs suspicious that 'new Presbyter is but old priest writ large'. Presbyterians claimed a divine right for their rule just as Laud had done for episcopacy.

By 1646 there was considerable demand outside Parliament for some degree of toleration. Already a number of gathered churches existed – for instance, in Norwich, Yarmouth, Bristol and Stepney. The army's decisive intervention in politics in June 1647 made its views henceforth of major significance. The month before this intervention *Grievances of the Regiments* were drawn up by the Agitators for presentation to the Parliamentary commissioners at Saffron Walden on 13–14 May.

EXERCISE

Read the extract from these grievances in your Anthology (extract 87) and consider what the effects of these complaints would have been in the summer of 1647.

DISCUSSION

The Agitators complained that liberty of conscience and worship were still denied, although the war had been fought to remove episcopal oppression. They were making the novel demand that complete liberty of conscience should be recognized as one of the issues for which the Civil War had been fought, and they were aligning themselves with the sects.

In the summer of 1647 the generals, negotiating with the King separately from the Army Council, produced their own Heads of Proposals, which included proposals affecting the church. Look at these in the Anthology (extract 67). All coercive powers of bishops and church courts were to be taken away (which suggests the possibility of restoring some very modified form of episcopacy). All acts enjoining the use of the Book of Common Prayer and imposing penalties for non-attendance at church on Sundays were to be abolished. In another paragraph not included in the Anthology, the Instrument promised that 'the present unequal, troublesome and contentious way of ministers' maintenance by tithes' was 'to be considered of and some remedy applied'. (In 1650 Parliament did in fact abolish compulsory church attendance.)

But the King did not accept the Heads of Proposals, and they also came under attack from the Agitators in the New Model Army, as you will recall from your cassette of the Putney Debates. You are no doubt by now well acquainted with the Leveller alternative to the Heads of Proposals, the Agreement of the People (Anthology, extract 89). It declared that 'matters of religion and the ways of God's worship' were no concern even of the future, more democratic Representative which the Agreement hoped to set up. The most they would allow was that 'the public way of instructing the nation (so it be not compulsive) is referred to their discretion'. This envisaged the possibility of a continuing state church, but with no coercive powers whatsoever: something like the situation which prevails in England today. But the breach between Independents and Levellers in December 1648 put an end to these discussions.

The years 1649–53 saw no significant changes in the state church. The Presbyterian system set up in 1646 lost such coercive power as it had had: it continued to exist in some areas on a voluntary basis. Bishop's lands had been sold in 1646; dean and chapter lands followed in 1649. This made much more difficult any revival of limited episcopacy such as had been suggested in the Heads of Proposals. Financial needs and the pressure of the City were thus limiting factors from one side. From the other there were even stronger pressures from the gentry, and conservatives generally, for the preservation of a state church, with ministers maintained by tithes and appointed by lay patrons. Alderman Violet, indeed, thought this essential for the recovery of trade (see *C of R*, pages 140–1). These came to be the decisive issues dividing conservatives from radicals.

The early fifties also witnessed a debate about the nature of the ministry, and indeed about the desirability of having a settled ministry at all.

EXERCISE

Read extracts 70–5 in the Anthology, and try to work out what were the points of disagreement concerning (a) the relation of ministers to their congregations and (b) a state church. You will find more evidence about the differences in extracts 76–80.

DISCUSSION

Conservatives like Hall, Bourne and Baxter believed that a complete system of church government had been laid down in the Bible, the revealed Word of God. All that remained was to follow it. (Unfortunately they disagreed on what exactly Scripture said.) Such men thought ministers must be trained in universities to perform their pastoral functions adequately, that they should be settled in one congregation, and that they should receive adequate incomes in order to fulfil their pastoral functions without distraction. Immanuel Bourne among very many others believed that the clergy had a divine right to tithes.

Radicals like Walwyn, Hartley, Collier and Fox held on the contrary that God's will was revealed by the spirit working in believers' hearts as well as by the Bible, and that a call to preach came from God alone: no ordination and no university training were necessary. The Scriptures spoke for themselves to believers, and needed no learned interpreters. So the debate about the ministry called in question the function of the universities. (See Block 4, 'Education in England to 1660', and Dell, extract 107 in the Anthology.)

The conservative defence of the ministry aroused the intense hostility of such radicals as Levellers, Diggers and Ranters. They saw the established clergy in a very different light: as deceivers of the people, in alliance with social and political oppressors. The clergy are linked to the existing order by their vested interest in tithes (see Anthology, extracts 70–3, 77–8, and Block 5, 'Gerrard Winstanley'). For a Quaker like Nayler there is no need for a settled ministry; preachers are called like the disciples to give up everything for Christ. They should be supported by the people's donations, not by tithes. Lest we should dismiss such views as those of extremist agitators, it is worth remembering that Milton had very similar ideas, which we shall be discussing in Block 7, *Milton and Marvell*.

Tithes concerned not only the clergy. Hated as an unpopular tax by middle and lower-class laymen, tithes were a very important source of income for the many propertied laymen who owned or leased them. Attempts by Archbishops Bancroft and Laud earlier in the century to recover for the church tithes impropriated at the dissolution of the monasteries in the fifteen-thirties had been foiled by gentry opposition. Any proposal to abolish tithes or lay patronage looked like an attack on property. Many even among the Independents (including the army grandees) could not conceive of a society without a state church and a settled and maintained ministry. They sought to preserve lay patronage rights and the property rights of lay impropriators. Within these limits they were prepared to be much more tolerant than episcopalians or Presbyterians. But the limitations severed them from sectaries, the religious radicals.

A confrontation came in the Barebones Parliament of 1653, which passed a bill for the abolition of lay patronage and voted (by a narrow majority) against the retention of tithes (see *C of R*, page 114). The conservatives in the House got together and handed their power back to Oliver Cromwell. Look again at the extracts from Josselin's Diary in your Anthology, extract 61: they reveal his anxieties on the subject of tithes.

Oliver Cromwell himself had considerable sympathy for demands for liberty of conscience and worship. But he also had the social conservatism of a gentleman, a great respect for existing property rights. At the same time he wanted to preserve a national, all-inclusive state church in order to give the Protectorate a broad basis of support as well as conserving unity among the revolutionaries. Unfortunately this sensible idea ran up against the social anxieties of the gentry, as you can hear from the Nayler debates (Cassette 4).

We could almost decipher the growing conservatism of the fifties from the history of tithes. The Instrument of Government of December 1653, which set up the Protectorate, made a last attempt to square the circle. (Read its religious clauses carefully: Anthology, extract 68.) Reflecting the strong feeling against tithes which still existed in the army, it proposed that 'as soon as may be, a provision less subject to scruple and contention, and more certain', should be substituted. Those last three words, and the constitution's insistence that a state church should be maintained, were intended to reassure conservatives that no precipitate action was intended. The Parliament of 1654–5, however, was not satisfied. Its proposed constitution insisted that 'until some better provision be made *by the Parliament*' (my italics), the present maintenance should be retained. This was a very satisfactory formula, since the apparent hopes of change which it held out to the radicals would never be realized 'by the Parliament'. Two years later the Petition and Advice went further still: it assumed the continuance of tithes, insisting now that they should go only to ministers of whose orthodoxy Parliament approved. Only after the breakdown of 1659 did tithes again seem to be threatened, by agitation headed by the Quakers. Milton published his most powerful indictment, *Considerations touching the Likeliest Means to Remove Hirelings out of the Church*, in May 1659. A year later King and bishops returned; tithes and impropriations were saved. (See Block 8, *The Restoration*.)

With hindsight we may well think that the maintenance of a tithe-supported ministry and of lay patronage so divided the revolutionaries as ultimately to make the Restoration inevitable. Yet the Cromwellian state church deserves our serious examination. The Instrument of Government insisted that although 'the Christian religion as contained in the Scriptures' should 'be held forth and recommended as the public profession of these nations', yet 'none shall be compelled by penalties or otherwise', provided they 'abuse not this liberty to the civil injury of others and to the actual disturbance of the public peace', and provided this liberty did not extend 'to Popery or Prelacy [i.e. irreconcilable episcopalians] nor to such as under the profession of Christ hold forth and practice licentiousness'. All laws contrary to this liberty of conscience were annulled, though not all JPs acted as if they were aware of the fact.

Thus, although liberty was restricted to 'such as profess faith in God by Jesus Christ', it was – in theory at least – pretty wide by seventeenth-century standards. The formula did not necessarily exclude even anti-Trinitarians like Milton. The public profession of 'the Christian religion as contained in the Scriptures' allowed very considerable varieties of interpretation. Papists and prelatists were excluded for political rather than religious reasons; provided they did not indulge in plots, they continued to enjoy toleration in fact.

There was a real prospect that all but the Laudian hard core of former episcopalians might in time have been reconciled to the Cromwellian church. Although bishops continued – illegally – to ordain priests, no new bishops were consecrated, and there was real concern towards the end of the fifties lest the apostolic succession might run out. There were no risks in tolerating such an ill-organized and divided group. The Catholic community also benefited from Cromwell's rule. Some twenty-one priests were executed under the Commonwealth: only two under the Protectorate. A law insisting that Catholics must abjure the Pope was never enforced. Catholics and Laudians could be tolerated so long as they were politically inactive. This relatively tolerant attitude did not extend, of course, to the Catholic majority of the population of Ireland.

But the Cromwellian church also included more radical Protestants. There were Independent ministers, who in theory believed that church and state should be separate, who yet felt that they could hold office within the national church. They ministered both to their own gathered churches of saints and to the entire parish. This happened in Ralph Josselin's parish of Earls Colne, Essex (see the relevant extracts from his Diary in the Anthology, extract 61). Many other ministers would not accept parochial cures within the national church, but felt able to take town or cathedral lectureships, or university appointments. Separatist congregations were also tolerated on the periphery of the national church: for example, radical Arminians under John Goodwin in London; Baptist churches in Bristol, Fenstanton and Hexham. The Baptists even began to organize themselves, the General Baptists nationally, the Particular Baptists on regional lines.

EXERCISE

Read the extracts from Cromwell's speeches in the Anthology (extracts 98–100). Why do you suppose he favoured such a broadly-based national church?

DISCUSSION

Whatever one's view of Cromwell's personal commitment to toleration (whether, for example, he saw it as the *right* of the individual, as did the Levellers), one is forced to conclude that he was also influenced by the political need to create a broad basis of support for his rule. Conservatives whose active support could not be enlisted must be encouraged to work for compromise rather than confrontation. The sects must not be goaded into revolt because the rule of the saints had not been inaugurated, or because Cromwell had failed to honour what both George Fox and Henry Jessey regarded as his promise to abolish tithes. Within these limits toleration would be extended to all law-abiding religious bodies and individuals outside the national church. But 'law-abiding' begged a lot of questions. Many Quakers thought it their religious duty to break the law by disrupting services of the national church.

Cromwell's church embraced so many different opinions, and was so uncoercive, that Presbyterians and other conservatives were tempted to ask, was it a state church at all, or mere anarchy? *C of R* summarizes such views: 'it had no discipline, no courts. A horrid vacuum remained. There was a grave danger that the lower orders might be able to do what they liked, within the limits of the common law' (page 147). Cromwell's church was comprehensive because it had no definition, no structure. Many Presbyterians, Independents and Episcopalians were distressed by a church which tolerated so much and offered no discipline. They wanted ministers (in the absence of church courts) to have the right to exclude men and women from the sacraments, as an instrument of control and discipline. They also wanted state intervention to prevent hecklers interrupting their services. Radicals, on the other hand, disapproved on principle of any church whose authority was enforced by the state, even a church so much more loosely organized and tolerant than the Laudian and Presbyterian versions of the Anglican church. So Cromwell had to perform a balancing trick – placating his new conservative allies whilst still extending practical toleration to his old sectarian allies.

In December 1656 the Quaker leader, James Nayler, was charged in Parliament with blasphemy, in that 'he assumed the gesture, words, names and attributes of our Saviour Christ'. The issues were many: should Parliament try Nayler for the alleged offence or leave his case to due process of law? Was Nayler really claiming *to be* the Messiah, or was he acting out a sign only? If he was guilty of the ultimate blasphemy, could this be tolerated? How far should the Quakers as a sect be tolerated? If Nayler was to be punished, how? – death, banishment, or something else?

EXERCISE

Listen to the extracts from the Nayler Debate on Cassette 4. What answers were given to the questions posed in the preceding paragraph? How were they countered?

DISCUSSION

Do not concern yourself with the details of the case. What matters is the depth of feeling evident in the speeches made against Nayler and against the Quakers as a group. Several points may be noted, over and above Nayler's alleged offence of impersonating Christ.

1   Nayler's opponents are querying the whole policy of religious toleration.

2   The political context is inextricable from the religious. The Quakers were feared as a seditious sect. Skippon says, 'Their great growth and increase is too notorious, both in England and Ireland; their principles strike both at ministry and magistracy'. This panic surprises us, because we think of the later Quakers as pacifists. But Quakers in the sixteen-fifties were not all pacifists. Nayler's writings included in the Anthology show a millenarian desire to inaugurate the rule of the saints; compare this with Immanuel Bourne's incitement of Cromwell against the Quakers (extract 79). So Nayler's opponents were not only objecting to a specific instance of alleged blasphemy but to its social implications. (Cf. Cassette 3, *The Lamb's Officer*.)

3   There is an important debate about the legal situation which even calls in question the legal basis of the Instrument of Government. But was there any law at all if the Instrument was not legal? Could Parliament try Nayler, or indeed anyone? Traditionally, only the House of Lords had judicial powers; and it had been abolished in 1649. The Lord Chief Justice claims that 'whatsoever authority was in the Houses of Lords and Commons, is united in this Parliament'. But some MPs denied this: it had never been formally enacted. In an attempt to sidestep the issue, Major Beake (in a passage not quoted on cassette) said, 'I conceive the judgement of Parliament is so sovereign that it may declare that to be an offence which never was an offence'. Others

Figure 3 James Nayler (1617?–60) branded with a 'B' for blasphemer. Engraving by unknown artist for Ephraim Pagit, Heresiography: or a discription of the heretickes of these latter times, *5th edition, 1654. (Mansell Collection.)*

IAMES NAYLOR

Of all the Sects that Night, and Errors own
And with false Lights possess the world, ther's none
More strongly blind, or who more madly place
The light of Nature for the light of Grace.

replied that Parliament is not a court of first instance (and therefore cannot try Nayler), but can act only by legislation. And then as Sydenham put it, 'to take away a man's life by a subsequesnt law, it is a dangerous consequence . . . It may be any man's case, hereafter, to be accused for an offence, and from the bare report of a [Parliamentary] committee to have the sentence of death passed upon him without further hearing'.

4   There is the issue of the penalty to be imposed. In the end Nayler was not executed or banished: he was flogged, branded and maimed – so violently that he died shortly afterwards.

Cromwell did not intervene to prevent Parliament carrying out its savage sentence; but he subsequently challenged their authority for doing so. There can be little doubt that he disliked the precedent which Parliament's actions set. As he pointed out to a meeting of army officers, 'the case of James Nayler might happen to be your own case'. Yet Cromwell could not continue a policy of complete toleration in the face of such fierce opposition from the 'natural rulers' with whom he wanted to come to terms. He used the occasion to suggest the need for a second chamber to balance the Commons. The Humble Petition and Advice was the outcome.

One cannot help sympathizing with Cromwell's impatient reaction to the wranglings of the radicals in face of this determined attack on the whole policy of religious toleration by the 'natural rulers' and their Parliament. 'When shall we have men of a universal spirit?', he asked. 'Everyone desires to have liberty, but none will give it'. 'Nothing will satisfy them unless they can put their finger upon their brethren's consciences, to pinch them there'. What was later to be called 'the dissidence of dissent' facilitated the religious reaction which Cromwell had reluctantly to accept in the Petition and Advice of 1657, and ultimately it did much to bring about the defeat of the revolutionary cause.

But what was actually done for the clergy? Tithes were retained. The incomes of poorer clergymen were augmented by state grants, and by encouraging Royalist delinquents to pay part of their fines by settling impropriated tithes on the local parson. In some areas small parishes were united, large ones sub-divided to meet population changes. (We discussed the need for this in Block 3, 'Calvinism, Arminianism and Counter-revolution'.) The clergy as a whole were better off in the sixteen-fifties than they had been earlier.

Lay patronage rights were untouched unless the patron was a delinquent: patronage formerly exercised by bishops and deans and chapter passed into lay hands. Under the Long Parliament County Committees appointed to livings of delinquent patrons, but usually consulted parishioners as to their wishes – an unofficial concession to the principle of popular election. Parishioners were able to appoint directly to livings formerly in the crown's patronage. But governments did attempt to assert some central control over the appointment of ministers. So long as it functioned, the Westminster Assembly examined candidates for ordination. In March 1654 the Commission for the Approbation of Public Preachers was set up, with lay and clerical members (commonly known as the Triers). This body acknowledged the rights of patrons, merely reserving the right (formerly belonging to the Archbishop of Canterbury and the King) of presenting to livings which had been left vacant for more than six months.

On the other hand, control over the conduct of the clergy was decentralized, the Ejectors working at county level. Cromwell tried to enlist the support of Presbyterians, Independents and Baptists as Triers and Ejectors: the Commissioners were acknowledged by these groups to be doing a good job. (Compare Baxter's verdict, quoted in *C of R*, page 147, with Bourne's gloomier view in the Anthology, extract 79.)

So Cromwell was trying to build up a comprehensive national church, with practical toleration outside it for peaceful Protestant sects and papists. He was pushed hard by his Parliament of 1656, which reintroduced compulsory church attendance (though with no machinery for enforcement comparable with that which had existed before 1640) and severely limited religious toleration by demanding a Confession of Faith which would have excluded anti-Trinitarians like Milton or (later) Sir Isaac Newton. Nevertheless, Cromwell's attempts achieved a limited success. Had he lived, his church might have lived with him, since it did not seriously impinge on the interests of the 'natural rulers' or the clergy. But in the two years after his death the radicals failed to agree on alternative policies, whilst terrifying gentry and clergy by their threatening attitude towards tithes, patronage and the state church. So bishops came back with Charles II, and Cromwell's interesting experiment – the first of its kind in Europe – was never properly tried out.

When we come to look at the post-Restoration settlement of the church, we shall find that it created a new division of Protestant Englishmen into two nations – separated not only by religious beliefs but also by educational opportunity. Some have described this as a tragedy for English cultural life, whose consequences have not yet been totally eradicated. It is something for you to think about.

Millenarianism and Fifth Monarchism

(Start by reading or rereading *C of R*, pages 143–5.)

When we think of millenarian ideas in the seventeenth century, we should very carefully clear our minds of the rather cranky associations of the ideas in our own day. In the seventeenth century the Bible was still believed to be the source of all truth. Prophecies of the end of the world are to be found scattered throughout the Bible. Some of the best scholarly minds in Europe applied themselves to interpreting the prophecies, no doubt stimulated by the crises which affected all Europe in the sixteenth and seventeenth centuries, and which seemed to be ushering in either something new and unprecedented or – more probably – the end of the world.

Interpreting the prophecies in Daniel and Revelation was especially the sphere of mathematicians, from John Napier, who invented logarithms at the end of the sixteenth century, to Sir Isaac Newton at the end of the seventeenth (see Anthology extracts 146–51 for Newton's writings). Such men hoped to establish a science of prophecy, just as Hobbes and Harrington believed in the possibility of establishing a science of politics. Neither hope was realized, but by the sixteen-forties a scholarly consensus seemed to have established, on the basis of these mathematical studies, an agreed interpretation of Biblical prophecy. The four monarchies of Babylon, Persia, Greece and Rome had ended; the fifth monarchy of Christ was imminent. Significant events, including the fall of Antichrist, the conversion of the Jews, and perhaps Christ's Second Coming itself were likely to occur in the sixteen-fifties or, at the latest, the sixteen-nineties. In the millennium Christ and his saints would rule on earth for a thousand years.

Writings of this sort were not allowed to be published under the Laudian censorship. But when censorship broke down after 1640 there was a rush of publications – translations and popular summaries of learned Latin works by John Napier, Thomas Brightman, John Henry Alsted and Joseph Mede, a Fellow of Milton's college at Cambridge. Mede's treatise was published on the orders of the House of Commons, translated by an MP, with a Preface by William Twisse, Presbyterian minister and Prolocutor (speaker) of Parliament's Assembly of Divines. In this semi-official publication Twisse observed, in Baconian vein, that the opening of the world by navigation and commerce coincided in time with an increase of scientific and Biblical knowledge.

Little imagination is needed to realize the effect of these writings, suddenly made accessible, in a world where established certainties were breaking down, where almost anything seemed possible. John Milton in 1641–2 spoke of Christ as 'shortly-expected king', whose kingdom was 'now at hand'. Some extremists even considered that since Christ's kingdom was about to be established, all earthly power which might obstruct it must be rejected, nay overthrown. Most Protestants had long thought that the Pope was Antichrist, whose fall was a necessary precondition of the millennium. But an even longer-standing heretical tradition asserted that bishops and the whole hierarchy of the established church were antichristian. This belief resurfaced in the freedom of the sixteen-forties. The fall of the Laudian bishops, and their association in Puritan eyes with popery, opened up vast possibilities to Parliamentarian propagandists when they had to drum up recruits and support for the war against the King. Pulpits rang with appeals to 'you that are of the meaner rank, common people' to fight the Lord's battles against Antichrist. Hence the importance of stressing that Charles I was supported by papists, in England, in Ireland and abroad: the Royalists were 'the antichristian party'.

Such arguments drew upon the radical Protestant tradition summed up in Foxe's *Book of Martyrs*. All history was depicted as a struggle between right and wrong, between Christ and Antichrist, with God's Englishmen foremost in the good fight. The fact that the Lollards and the Marian martyrs whose fate Foxe so graphically depicted had mainly been artisans gave a 'democratic' twist to his story: the most determined foes of Antichrist were the common people. Despite (or because of) the fact that Laud would not allow the *Book of Martyrs* to be reprinted, Foxe was very widely read and known: he is the only author apart from the Bible whom Winstanley quotes. Foxe's myth fitted perfectly into the ideological demands of Parliamentarian propaganda in the Civil War: the King, the prelates and the nobility were Antichrist's servants. 'The voice that will come of Christ's reigning', announced a Puritan divine (probably Thomas Goodwin) in 1641, 'is like to begin from those that are the multitude, that are so contemptible, especially in the eyes and account of Antichrist's spirits and the prelacy'. Goodwin believed that 'the last times' would begin in 1650. With utopian enthusiasm and confident energy preachers and pamphleteers hammered the theme home.

Some of the common people took the preachers' exhortations very seriously. 'The vox populi', declared Stephan Marshall in a sermon preached before the House of Commons in December 1641, 'is that many of the nobles, magistrates, knights and gentlemen, and persons of great quality, are arrant traitors and rebels against God'. A Puritan could hardly use stronger words. 'It is neither rebellion nor treason to fight for the King, to recover his power out of the hand of the Beast', said Francis Cheynell in 1643; and by fighting for the King he meant fighting for the King and Parliament *against* the King and 'the antichristian faction' which had seized the King's person. Parliamentarian soldiers taken prisoner in 1644 shocked a Royalist divine by arguing that they were 'the men that must help to pull' down Antichrist, in England here and now. Antichrist was in Rome, not England, Mr Symmons explained; and pulling him down was the job of kings, not of the common people. But his hearers were not convinced. They had the authority of John Goodwin, who had said in 1642 'now we know' that Antichrist 'is about to be destroyed and cast out of the world'; and that men 'of ordinary rank and quality' were to execute God's judgements.

It is important to realize that John and Thomas Goodwin and Francis Cheynell were not isolated extremists. 'The most of the chief divines' in London, the Scot Robert Baillie wrote in 1645, 'not only Independents but others . . . are express Chiliasts' (i.e. millenarians). So was John Milton. So perhaps was Cromwell: see his letter to Hammond, Anthology, extract 92; and look also at Keith Thomas on 'Providence' in your Reader (article 2). Cromwell's emphasis on 'providences' shows him trying to interpret the signs of the times in accordance with what he believed to be God's purposes for England, and to draw guidance for immediate action. John Cook, who presented the Commonwealth's case against Charles I at his trial, argued that the court which sentenced the King 'was a resemblance and representation of the great day of judgement, when the saints shall judge all wordly powers'. John Canne observed that the throne of God had been set up in England when Charles was condemned; soon, he predicted, it would be 'set up in other kingdoms . . . As monarchy falls, so falls antichristianism'. Again Milton agreed. (Milton's ideas are discussed in detail in Block 7, *Milton and Marvell*.)

To many indeed the execution of Charles in 1649 seemed to make sense only as clearing the way for King Jesus and the millennium. Between 1648 and 1651 Ralph Josselin – a relative conservative – read many millenarian tracts and was continually thinking and dreaming about the end of the world, though he did not share the popular view that this would happen in 1655 or 1656. (Look at the relevant extracts from his *Diary* in the Anthology, extract 61.) Oliver Cromwell's speech at the opening of the Barebones Parliament in July 1653 has millenarian overtones (see Anthology, extract 98). 'The Judgment Day is at hand', Bunyan announced in 1658. Edmund Ludlow's *A Voyce from the Watch Tower* makes it clear that many of the regicides executed in 1660 were still sustained by the millenarian conviction that they were co-operating with God's purposes which had given them courage to act in 1649 (see Anthology, extract 117). Nor were such expectations entertained only by men whose concerns were primarily other-worldly. A speaker in the Barebones Parliament thought it important that 'the seas should be secured . . . in order to prepare for the coming of Christ'. The author of *The Coming of Christs Appearing in Glory* knew 'of nothing more important than matters of trade, as tending to strengthen the position against all eventualities'.

Such expectations reached their zenith in the late sixteen-forties; the Fifth Monarchist movement which emerged after 1653 marked their decline. As the coming of Christ's kingdom was delayed, as life got no better for the common people, and especially with the manifest shift of power into more conservative hands after the dissolution of the Barebones Parliament, a Fifth Monarchist group emerged, determined to expedite the coming of the kingdom by military violence. 'Men variously impoverished by the long troubles', observed the mathematician John Pell in March 1655, 'full of discontents and tired by long expectation of amendment, must needs have great propensions to hearken to those that proclaim times of refreshing – a golden age – at hand'.

Interestingly enough, the Fifth Monarchist group shared – or inherited – many traditional Leveller positions, attacking a state church, tithes and lawyers as well as the rich. Dr Capp stresses their class consciousness, their hostility to aristocracy. John Rogers attacked 'naughty nobles' and 'profane and swaggering gentry'. Fifth Monarchists seem to have been strongest in towns and many of their rank-and-file members had connections with the clothing industry. In 1657 and 1661 plots by a small Fifth Monarchist group headed by Thomas Venner aimed at overthrowing the government, confiscating the estates of their enemies and putting them into a common treasury (see Anthology, extract 106). In 1661, under the slogan 'For King Jesus!', Venner's manifesto denounced 'the old, bloody, popish wicked gentry of the nation'. But even in the sixteen-fifties millenarianism was not restricted to Fifth Monarchists. It played a significant part in the early Quaker movement.

EXERCISE

Listen to George Fox's *The Lamb's Officer* on Cassette 3, and summarize in your own words what you think Fox is trying to say.

DISCUSSION

We think of the Quakers as pacifists who take no part in political activity. But Fox hardly fits that picture, does he? We recall that 'the peace principle' was not announced until after the restoration of Charles II in 1660. In 1659 many Quakers were politically active in defence of the republic. 'We look for a new earth as well as a new heaven', wrote the Quaker leader Edward Burrough in October 1659. (See 'Nonconformity' in Block 8, *The Restoration*.) Quakers revived the Leveller and Digger agitation against tithes and for law reform. They fiercely rejected a state church and demonstrated provocatively and fearlessly against it. The debates in Parliament on James Nayler show that many MPs regarded the Quakers as a serious social threat. We should not take Fox's military title and phraseology too literally: he is using the language of the Bible metaphorically. But it is hardly surprising that many of his contemporaries were very alarmed. They did not know, as we do, that the Quakers were not associated with the militant Fifth Monarchist movement; nor did they know that the latter anyway posed no serious threat to the social order.

For our purposes the key sentence is Fox's first: 'The Lord Jesus Christ is come to reign'. 'Now shall the Lamb and saints have victory', he added. The millennium is not something in the future: it is here. Consequently God's servants have the right to call priests to the bar of judgment, and magistrates, rulers and people as well. No wonder priests and magistrates did not like Quakers, who summoned them to judgment in the Lord's name.

As society seemed to be on the verge of another crisis in 1659, the millenarian hopes of the sixteen-forties revived. Only this time conservatives had learnt their lesson. Aware by now of the social threat underlying popular millenarianism, former Parliamentarians and former Royalists united to recall Charles II (this is discussed in more detail in 'Background to the Restoration', in Block 8, *The Restoration*).

Despite the fantastic courage of the handful of Fifth Monarchist rebels who terrorized the whole of London in 1661, despite the self-sacrificial determination with which Quakers continued to testify against tithes, that was the end. Christ's kingdom manifestly was not coming in England in the immediate future. Quaker pacifism originated at least in part in a desire to clear Friends of association with Fifth Monarchist revolts. But all those who had assumed that the millennium was at hand had to rethink their position. 'Take heed of computing', wrote John Owen in 1680; 'how woefully and wretchedly have we been mistaken by this'.

As the revolutionary crisis subsided, men realized that millenarianism could be adapted to conservative uses. Marvell in 1655 suggested that Oliver Cromwell's rule might be leading to the millennium, but at the same time he clearly repudiated revolutionary Fifth Monarchism. After the Restoration Dryden in *Annus Mirabilis* converted millenarianism to the uses of a monarchy which he believed would make England mistress of the trade of the world. In the long run this is perhaps the most interesting legacy of millenarianism – the hopes it raised for a *new* utopian future. Initially all the revolutionaries had looked for a revival of the past – Levellers for a recovery of Anglo-Saxon freedom, sectaries for a return of primitive Christianity, Diggers and Quakers for a recapture of Adam's state of innocence before the Fall. Millenarianism shifted the golden age to the future. Once it had shaken off its apocalyptic associations, it could easily link up with Bacon's scientific optimism to form a theory of progress.

After 1660 the revolutionary content of millenarianism, Milton's belief that Christ would come 'to put an end to all earthly tyrannies', faded away; increasingly predictions of the imminent end of the world are left to cranks. Isaac Newton, who still thought that 'the last age' was 'now approaching', went on secretly trying to solve the chronological problems of the Second Coming; but for others it receded further and further into the future, and ceased to be practical politics. When the Reverend John Mason proclaimed that Jesus Christ would appear visibly at Water Stratford on Whitsunday 1694 nobody in authority took him seriously. He was advised 'to let blood speedily'. In the eighteenth-century 'age of enlightenment' *secular* doctrines of progress came into vogue.

Further reading

W. M. Lamont (1969) *Godly Rule. Politics and Religion, 1603–60*, Macmillan.
B. S. Capp (1972) *The Fifth Monarchy Men: A Study in Seventeenth Century English Millenarianism*, Faber and Faber.

The Breakdown of Calvinism

(Start by reading or rereading *C of R*, pages 251–2.)

At the beginning of our period, Calvinism was the dominant theology even in the hierarchy of the Church of England. Archbishops Grindal (1575–83), Whitgift (1583–1604) and Abbott (1610–33) – and James I – were Calvinists. Calvinism was no monopoly of the Puritans, though the Laudians were soon to try to make it appear to be so. In the sixteen-forties the ideology of Calvinism seemed to be a revolutionary threat to church and state alike. Yet by the end of our period Calvinism was no longer the intellectual force it had been. It was not stressed by the official Church of England, though the 'Latitudinarians' who came to dominate the church had more in common with the earlier 'Puritans' than with Laudians. In the eighteenth century the 'old dissent' which consisted of Presbyterians and Independents, was still mainly Calvinist; though Arminianism and Unitarianism were to make inroads into its ranks. Calvinism survived among the Particular Baptists, the Muggletonians: it was no longer in the forefront of intellectual history, and certainly no longer a revolutionary force. What had happened? There were four main elements in the waning of Calvinism.

1   In the sixteen-twenties and thirties there had still been a sense of international brotherhood among Protestants. Englishmen demanded intervention on the Protestant side in the Thirty Years War; the Scots Presbyterians were 'our brethren of Scotland'. But by 1650 the Calvinist international had ceased to exist: foreign policy was no longer envisaged in religious terms. One might argue about how far religion had ever been a dominant consideration for governments; but certainly from the sixteen-twenties and thirties, when France first suppressed the liberties of the Huguenots at home and then intervened in the Thirty Years War on the 'Protestant' side, it became difficult to take seriously the religious motives which governments still from time to time cited. The Treaty of Westphalia which ended the Thirty Years War in 1648 was a wholly secular settlement. In 1650 Puritan England invaded Presbyterian Scotland. The Scots were brethren no longer. The three Anglo-Dutch Wars of the sixteen-fifties, sixties and seventies were fought between Europe's two leading Protestant powers; when England and Holland finally led a coalition against France after 1688 it included the Catholic Habsburgs. The epoch of religious wars was over.

2   The Laudian interlude in England perhaps derived some of its appeal from its assertion of England's independence of both internationals, the Roman Catholic and the Calvinist. As we saw in Block 3, Laud severed relations with the latter without establishing firm links with the former. His was a provincial insular creed. But a more important aspect of the appeal of Laudianism was its rejection not only of revolutionary Calvinism, but also of the high Calvinism of the universities, the arid intellectual discussion of the absolute decrees, of predestination, of assurance of salvation and the visibility of the elect. Even a relatively liberal minister like Thomas Shepard, who emigrated to New England in 1635, believed that only one out of a thousand human beings were saved. So what could preachers say to the other 999? God's decree was unchangeable, and bore no relation to human merits or efforts. High Calvinism of this brand could not be an evangelizing doctrine: there are many stories of men and women reduced to despair and even suicide by contemplating their probable eternal destiny. This Calvinism had come to lack all warmth and humanity: one can understand why young poets like Richard Crashawe (and Andrew Marvell for a short time) reacted from it to an emotional popery, why liberal intellectuals like John Hales and Lord Falkland reacted from it to a more liberal and rational theology.

3   When ordinary people broke into politics and theology in the sixteen-forties, they rather naturally had not much use for this narrowly orthodox

theology. The Calvinism which survived the discussions of the revolution was either the liberalized covenant theology of the school of William Perkins and John Preston (which taught that if you worried about your salvation you were probably saved), or the revolutionary Puritanism of the sects, with its stress on the godly remnant who wrestled with God for a blessing, on the solidarity against their worldly enemies of those who recognized one another as saints. Such a doctrine still excluded the possibility of democracy: the elect remained by definition a minority. Democratic theories were possible only for those who rejected Calvinism.

4 During the revolution Calvinism was tested and found wanting. The doctrines of the oligarchy of the elect and of the necessity of discipline came up against the newly liberated ideas of lower-class sectaries who rejected the law and discipline of the church. Before 1640 these had flourished underground among Familists and General Baptists: religious toleration and liberty of the press and discussion brought them to the surface. The dominance of Calvinism proved incompatible with religious toleration; but religious toleration was necessary if the Civil War was to be won. The Presbyterian discipline which the Assembly of Divines hoped to establish came up against the erastianism of men like John Selden and the Milton of *Areopagitica*. Once Parliament had challenged the Westminster Assembly to defend its position from the Bible, and clerics lost their position as sole arbiters, Calvinism was vulnerable to lay theological criticism. The Presbyterian church set up in 1646 remained a paper tiger. It disappointed conservatives in particular by its failure to impose discipline on the profane multitude, to preserve traditional moral standards against the antinomian questioning of Seekers and sectaries. 'If the elect are chosen from all eternity', Roger Crab asked, 'what do priests take our money for?' (For antinomianism see 'Winstanley' in Block 5 and 'Milton's Heresies' in Block 7.)

Thus Calvinism came under attack from many sides almost simultaneously – from Laudian 'Arminianism' with its emphasis on the sacraments and ceremonies of the church, and on priestly control; from the liberal intellectual 'Socinianism' of the Great Tew circle; from the radical Arminianism of the sects, which rejected a separate priesthood altogether, rejecting too the theology of Calvinism, the oligarchy of the elect and the predestination of the mass of mankind to eternal damnation. William Walwyn could not believe that men would be 'tormented for ever without end for a little time of sinning in this world'. Intellectuals like John Goodwin and Milton were outraged at the insult to human freedom which the eternal decrees perpetuated.

Once discipline had broken down, it could no longer be assumed that the elect could be known on earth, still less that they coincided with the propertied minority. The Protestant doctrine of the priesthood of all believers elevated the consciences of believers above the institutionalized church, and even above the letter of Scripture. So long as the main strength of Protestantism was among the burghers of cities like Geneva, Amsterdam, La Rochelle, London, this had created few problems. Their consciences knew that God favoured hard work, accumulation, respect for property, monogamy. The Presbyterian preachers in the City of London, Thomas Hobbes noted, 'did never inveigh against the lucrative vices of men of trade or handicraft'. But God said very different things to lower-class consciences. Mechanic preachers and yeomen Quakers were convinced that the holy spirit was within them (see Fox, Anthology, extract 78). Artisan Fifth Monarchists proclaimed that they were the saints who should rule. Ranters and Quakers rejected the discipline and controls both of the Presbyterian church and of the Calvinist sects; their reliance on the inner light seemed subversive of all society's accepted moral standards. The radicals rejected as hypocrites those Puritans whose faith did not result in works of love. (The point is made by Fox in *The Lamb's Officer* on Cassette 3.) Sin began to lose its power as the great deterrent. The rise of democratic theories was accompanied by a questioning of belief in hell (Walker, *The Decline of Hell*, passim).

34

Ultimately a reaction came against the 'excesses' of the radicals, against the disruption of services by Quakers and their attempt (with which Milton sympathized) to abolish tithes. Conservatives came to feel that a state church, tithes and the patronage system must be preserved at all costs. The Presbyterian church of 1646 was a non-starter. Cromwell's state church of the fifties, interesting in its oecumenicism, allowed too much toleration to the radicals, and had none of the legal and emotional appeal of tradition. So in 1660 the episcopal church was restored, subordinate to Parliament, without Laudianism, and without a High Commission to rouse fears of clerical control. The theology of this church, if theology is not too strong a word, was neither Calvinsist nor Laudian, notwithstanding the success of individual Laudians in winning positions of authority in the restored hierarchy. The dominant group came to be composed of 'Latitudinarians', men who had conformed to the Cromwellian state church and now to the episcopal, men from whom the staunchest defenders of the Royal Society were drawn, men of moderation and latitude, tolerant within limits (though not to Quakers or other social subversives), emphasizing moral conduct rather than theological niceties, emphasizing too the usefulness of church to state. Marvell rather maliciously quoted Samuel Parker (later a bishop) as saying 'Put the case, the clergy were cheats and jugglers, yet it must be allowed they are necessary instruments of the state to awe the common people into fear and obedience, because nothing else can so effectively enslave them [here Marvell interjects – ' 'tis this it seems our author would be at!'] as the fear of invisible power and the dismal apprehensions of the world to come'. Church courts came to concern themselves mainly with chivvying dissenters; the social and moral control which had previously been their function was taken over (increasingly from the sixteen-eighties) by JPs.

The disintegration of Calvinism led to a revival of the doctrine of justification by works – 'by their fruits ye shall know them'. Standards and norms of conduct could be established by JPs, with no danger of a clerical discipline, Laudian or Presbyterian. For the defeated, disillusioned sectaries too, Calvinism lost much of its driving force after 1660. One could make great sacrifices so long as one believed they were necessary to bring about God's kingdom on earth. But once this hope had been abandoned, once the sinfulness of man had again been accepted, the sects themselves co-operated in enforcing a morality of works on their members. Excommunication played a large part in the proceedings of non-conformist sects, but it was effective only in so far as it was accepted by the members of the congregation, or could be enforced by giving or withholding poor relief.

But this 'Arminian' theology of works is something entirely different from the Catholic or Laudian theology, whose works had been exclusively associated with the ceremonies and sacraments of the church, with the mediating priesthood. Protestantism, with its emphasis on the individual conscience and individual study and interpretation of the Scriptures, had aspired to internalize moral standards. No doubt it had not been entirely successful so far as the mass of the population was concerned: its failure in this respect appalled Milton. But in so far as standards were enforced at the end of our period, it was done not by confession and absolution, not by the economic sanctions of church courts, but either by the individual conscience, or by the voluntary discipline of the sectarian congregation, or by JPs, or by the voluntary societies for the Reformation of Manners.

Calvinism became a shibboleth, a loyalty to hold on to in a hostile world, no longer a dynamic force to change that world. We are all so much Arminians now that it requires a great imaginative effort to think ourselves back into the pre-revolutionary society which Calvinism dominated, a more magical society than anything we have ever known. It was yet another route by which traditional Christian orthodoxy passed into deism, magic into something more like science, morals and conduct became more important than theology. The 'old dissent' became increasingly passive politically, turned its energies – which had always been this-wordly – to economic matters, in which the solidarity of the sect proved very helpful, and to scientific enquiry. But as it turned away from politics, as Christ's kingdom was recognized not to be of this world, so emphasis on the after life was enhanced.

Reference

D. P. Walker (1964) *The Decline of Hell: Seventeenth Century Discussions of Eternal Torment,* Chicago University Press.

Further reading

G. R. Cragg (1950) *From Puritanism to the Age of Reason: A Study of Changes in Religious Thought within the Church of England, 1660 to 1700,* Cambridge University Press.

K. V. Thomas (1973) *Religion and the Decline of Magic,* Penguin, Chapters 2–6.

Protestantism, Puritanism and Science

Contents

Protestantism, Puritanism and Science

Before you start you should reread *C of R*, pages 15–6, 212–13, 260–1 and 267–8. Look also at Keith Thomas in the Reader, articles 2 and 3. It might help to reread 'Politics in a Changing Society' in Block 1. As you work through, you should bear in mind, and if necessary refer back to, Colin Chant's discussion of Francis Bacon in Block 3, *A Divided Society*. Many of the points which I make about the scientific revolution and the Royal Society are developed in Noel Coley's 'The Royal Society' in Block 8, *The Restoration*.

Introduction: Protestantism and capitalism

If you look at pages 77–80 of *C of R* you will find some suggestions about connections between Protestantism, Puritanism and the rise of modern science. This is another controversial subject. It relates to an analogous controversy over Protestantism and the origins of capitalism. Since the seventeenth century very many observers have noted that capitalism developed earliest and fastest in the Protestant countries, especially in the Netherlands and England. In 1668 an old City republican, Slingsby Bethel, took for granted the economic inferiority of popery and listed five reasons: nuns, monks and friars are removed from productive economic activity; a celibate clergy means a declining population; superstition leads to extravagance in adorning churches and to too many holidays; pilgrimages waste working time; begging orders live on the alms of the poor. (You will come across Bethel, caricatured as Shimei, in Dryden's *Absalom and Achitophel*; see Anthology, extract 134.)

Historians and sociologists disagree about the nature of the connection between Protestantism and the rise of capitalism, but only a few eccentrics would suggest that there is no connection of any sort. Max Weber, reacting against Marx's emphasis on the primacy of economics, argued (in *The Protestant Ethic and the Spirit of Capitalism*, 1930) that Protestantism and especially Calvinism led to a 'spirit of capitalism', an emphasis on serving God in one's calling, which came to justify the making of profits and the accumulation of capital. R. H. Tawney in *Religion and the Rise of Capitalism*, a book that you should read if possible, pointed out that most of Weber's evidence for 'the capitalist spirit' came from the seventeenth century. If we see 'the Protestant ethic' as a cause of the rise of capitalism, we have to account for the rise of the Protestant ethic. Men found it in the Bible, of course; but why did they find it there in the sixteenth century and not earlier? There are many convergent causes which explain the rise of capitalism – the discovery of America and the plunder of its gold and silver, the opening up of new sea routes to the East, the sixteenth-century inflation, the emergence of national states, expensive developments of warfare, an increase in population, the invention of printing, and a host of others. Chronologically it is easier to see capitalism as a contributory cause to the Protestant ethic than to see Protestantism as a cause of capitalism. So Tawney reversed Weber's causal order by suggesting that the Protestant and Puritan thinkers whom Weber cited were adapting themselves to the demands of a capitalist society already in existence, but which their theology helped to legitimate. This escapes from a difficulty which Weber never really faced – the existence of strong Calvinist churches in countries like Hungary and Scotland, which can by no stretch of the imagination be called capitalist in the sixteenth and seventeenth centuries.

Tawney's version avoids the absurdity of *equating* Protestantism and capitalism: Protestantism can exist without capitalism, just as capitalism can exist without Protestantism. But some of the emphases of Protestantism made it a theology which adapted more easily to a changing social environment than traditional Catholicism. What are these emphases?

Protestants stress the direct relationship between man and God, abolishing mediators between the two, whether the Virgin and the saints in heaven or the hierarchy of the church and its priesthood on earth. God speaks directly to the individual conscience; in the last resort the strongly held belief of the individual is superior to the authority of the church and its law; it can determine what he reads into the Bible. If you think about it, you can see how such doctrines can easily adapt to a changing social environment. For individual consciences do not exist in isolation from society: what a man believes to be right bears some relation to the society in which he lives. Early Protestantism established itself most securely in German towns, in the Netherlands, Geneva, La Rochelle, London. And it established itself most strongly among the educated laity of those commercial centres. When men in such places studied the Bible and their own consciences, they found there considerable tolerance for commercial practices condemned by the Catholic church. Calvin abandoned the church's absolute condemnation of usury. The Roman church had condemned it in theory but found all sorts of ways of condoning it in practice. Calvin's approach was much more straightforward: the individual conscience could overrule the law of the church. So an end was put to the hypocrisies and humbug of much traditional 'casuistry' on the subject.

Protestantism and science

The relationship between Protestantism and the rise of modern science is analogous to that between Protestantism and the rise of capitalism: only no one has yet suggested that 'the spirit of science' is an essential part of Protestantism! R. K. Merton's 'Science, Technology and Society in Seventeenth Century England' started a great discussion. You will notice that religion is not mentioned in Merton's title, and he devoted less than a third of his treatise to the links between Protestantism and science. He was at least equally concerned to emphasize the importance of contemporary economic developments – in mining, navigation and armaments industries – for the development of modern science. But – as with the parallel between Protestantism and capitalism – the parallel between science and Protestantism had been noted by contemporaries. The first historian of the Royal Society, Thomas Sprat, in 1667 compared the scientific revolution to the Protestant Reformation (Anthology, extract 140) and he had been anticipated not only by Francis Bacon but also by the Paracelsian chemist Richard Bostocke, who in 1585 compared the Copernican revolution in astronomy and the Paracelsian revolution in chemical medicine to the Protestant Reformation. (For Paracelsus, who hoped by drawing on the experience of craftsmen to found a new science of alchemy/chemistry, see Colin Chant, 'Francis Bacon', pages 35–6 in Block 3.)

Geographical facts suggest a similar analogy. Down to the sixteenth century Italy had been Europe's most advanced country, in science as in economics. But as the Counter-Reformation gathered strength, Italian scientists lost their pre-emenince. The republic of Venice, with its famous and liberal University of Padua, held out longest; but the condemnation of Galileo in 1633 marked a turning-point. Spain had already fallen out of the race. In the seventeenth century the Protestant Netherlands and Protestant England took the lead. A chemical physician, Theodore Mayerne – himself a Protestant by origin – was condemned in Paris and emigrated to London, where he prospered. Descartes left France for the safety of the Netherlands; even so, much of his scientific work was unpublished and he disguised his real beliefs in what he did print. Yet it did not prevent his writings being placed on the papal Index of Prohibited Books, where they remained until the present century. All books advocating the Copernican theory in astronomy in our period were placed on the Index. Increasingly, Italian and French scientists with unorthodox ideas had to publish in the Netherlands or England: the relative freedom of the press in Protestant countries was one of the ways in which the Reformation most benefited science. Isaac Newton was congratulated on having been born an Englishman, not afraid of the Inquisition like Galileo, nor compelled to publish abroad and to accommodate his philosophy to papal dogma like Descartes. Down to the present century the number of eminent scientists originating from Protestant countries greatly exceeded the number from Catholic countries.

But if Protestant countries were more favourable to science, England before 1640 with its episcopal state church occupied a half-way position between the more tolerant Netherlands and the Catholic countries; and the monarchy to some degree protected the monopoly of a corporation like the College of Physicians, which was deeply committed to traditional Galenic medicine. The censorship was being tightened up in early seventeenth-century England. In 1608 we find the great mathematician Thomas Hariot writing to the astronomer Kepler: 'Things with us are in such a condition that I cannot philosophize freely. We are still stuck in the mud. I hope Almighty God will soon put an end to it'. Similarly, before 1640 the Universities of Oxford and Cambridge were wedded to traditional Greek and Latin authorities, and were also dominated by the hierarchy of the church; science seems to have received little official encouragement, though it was a possible spare-time activity. But the universities were primarily institutions for training the clergy; before 1640 science, mathematics and medicine prospered most among the laity and especially in London, among physicians, surgeons, apothecaries, navigators, surveyors, etc. (See 'Education in England to 1660' in Block 4.)

But we must not oversimplify. We are talking of statistical trends, to which individual exceptions can always be found. There were scientists in the Catholic countries in the seventeenth century: historians have even located Laudian scientists. Many Protestants, especially among the clergy, were authoritarian and disliked the discussion of ideas which appeared to challenge what the text of the Bible stated. In the sixteenth century there had been many conflicts over translations into the vernacular – first of the Scriptures, then of scientific treatises. A group of Elizabeth's advisers, headed by the Earl of Leicester, a patron of Puritans, protected the translators of scientific books against their foes in the universities. But as late as 1649 Nicholas Culpeper complained that 'the College of Physicians will not suffer . . . physic to be printed in our mother tongue', upon the same grounds as led papists to forbid vernacular translations of the Bible. He utilized the new freedom of the press to publish English translations of the College of Physicians' private remedies so that they should be available to the poor as well as to the rich.

There was indeed a fundamental dilemma facing Protestants, which was never completely resolved. If there was to be a single state church – and this was long held to be essential if national unity and the existing social order were to be preserved – could full liberty of conscience and discussion be allowed? What was later called the 'dissidence of dissent', the readiness of other men's consciences to disagree with the consciences even of those who had liberated them from tyranny, was visible from the fifteen-twenties when Luther was outraged by peasants and Anabaptists appealing to his principles to justify their revolt.

The ideological significance of science

It is difficult but essential for us to realize the ideological significance of science in the seventeenth century. The nearest modern example I can think of is genetics, or atomic energy. A scientist today, however austere his scientific training, cannot ignore the political and social implications of these areas of science. Atomic energy can be used to destroy the human race; genetics raises questions of race relations, human equality, equality of education and of opportunity; so far-reaching are the implications of genetic research that one English geneticist, Sir Cyril Burt, working between the wars, is alleged to have invented evidence to support his conclusions. In the seventeenth century scientists were always in danger of running up against ideological taboos. The Bible was believed to be the source of all truth: the Bible said that Joshua told the sun to stand still. So how could the Copernican theory that the earth went round the sun be true? The period had inherited a habit of arguing by analogy, from the macrocosm to the microcosm. The king was to his kingdom as the sun was to the heavens or the heart to the body. But William Harvey, who had used the analogy in the dedication of his book on the circulation of the blood to Charles I in 1628, had second thoughts after the King had been executed. He explicitly rejected the analogy with the sun, and suggested that the blood was superior to and senior to the heart. No wonder he was accused of 'dethroning the heart', of being a 'seditious citizen of the physical commonwealth'.

The seventeenth century has been described as the period of 'the mechanization of the world picture'. The universe ceased to be 'animist', ceased to be filled with angels moving the heavenly spheres, or 'spirits' moving the blood in the human body. Motion began to be explained in terms of mechanical causation. But what seems to us now a simple 'common-sense' assumption upset a number of ideological apple-carts in the seventeenth century. If matter could move itself, if the planets and the blood were not pushed around, would not this diminish the power and authority of God? Or what if spirits, and the soul, and witches, did not exist? Before long, Sir Thomas Browne and Fellows of the Royal Society were defending the existence of witches as something necessary to belief in the existence of God.

Ancients against moderns

Half-way houses were found. Calvin, for instance, adopted St Augustine's view that the Bible had been written to the capacity of its readers, and must be interpreted in that light. This proved very useful for astronomers worried about Joshua and the sun. But it opened up other problems. It suggested that men had been simpler in the past, but now were wiser: that is to say, that the Moderns were better than the Ancients. This touched on a controversy which divided the intellectual world in the seventeenth century, with Bacon defending the Moderns and rejecting a whole series of traditional classical authorities. This seemed highly dangerous to conservatives. Aquinas had made Aristotle almost a Father of the Christian church. Harvey was very apologetic when, in demonstrating the circulation of the blood, he had to criticize Aristotle. Physicians who rejected the authority of Galen were liable to be fined by Harvey as Censor of the College of Physicians, and a major obstacle to acceptance of the Copernican astronomy was the Roman Catholic church's commitment to the geocentric system of Ptolemy. Oxford and Cambridge in particular, with their strong emphasis on the teaching of the classics, did not wish to see the authority of the Ancients lessened. This became a burning issue among those who wished to reform the universities in the sixteen-fifties.

But long before that positions had polarized. George Hakewill in 1627 published a large-scale defence of what seems to us the self-evident proposition that although the Ancients were giants, still the Moderns who stood on their shoulders might see further. He was fiercely attacked by Godfrey Goodman, Bishop of Gloucester, on specifically political and social grounds. 'If we be so meanly and basely persuaded of the Ancients, how apt shall we be for innovation, what danger of a mutiny; the country boors may rise in sedition, and not without cause; for by your opinion all things may be improved'. We smile when we read such a blimpish passage; but Goodman, who survived to see the 'country boors' in action in the sixteen-forties, and to see episcopacy abolished, probably thought that these events demonstrated his foresight.

In the long run Goodman was fighting a losing battle. But in the England of the sixteen-twenties and thirties, with a strict censorship to protect the interests of the old order, he had the big battalions on his side. A dashing young intellectual like Milton might shock Cambridge by defending the Moderns against the Ancients; and in 1638 another young Puritan declared that it was the devil who persuaded mankind to believe that novelty was a sign of error. His name was John Wilkins, whose professional career began as chaplain to Lord Saye and Sele, a leader of the Puritan and Parliamentarian opposition to Charles I. In 1645 Wilkins's *The Beauty of Providence* was, in Charles Webster's words, 'an updated, more concise and popular exposition of the work of Hakewill' (*The Great Instauration*, page 29). Wilkins went on to marry Oliver Cromwell's sister and to be one of Richard Cromwell's leading advisers in 1658–9. He conformed to the Anglican church in 1660, and became a bishop as well as father of the Royal Society. His approval of novelty had been repeated meanwhile by many who would never become bishops, including John Milton and Gerrard Winstanley. (For Wilkins see Sprat and Hooke in the Anthology, extracts 137–8 and 144.)

Science and magic

But the origins of modern science are more complicated than early historians of science used to think when they traced 'truths' evolving from one experiment to another. We know now that the 'mechanical philosophy' was to triumph over the animistic universe, and that natural magic, alchemy and astrology would sink to the status of pseudo-sciences. But this was not certain at the beginning of our period. Astrology and astronomy were virtually indistinguishable; those now regarded as the predecessors of modern chemistry were mostly alchemists. Philosophers like Giordano Bruno and Robert Fludd aspired to create a world view which would embrace natural magic as well as the latest scientific discoveries. The chemical medicine of Paracelsus and Van Helmont seemed likely to prevail until Boyle evolved his 'corpuscularian' philosophy. Most continental Paracelsians in the sixteenth and early seventeenth centuries were Calvinists (like Mayerne). It was Protestant religious exiles from Mary's persecution in the mid-sixteenth century who brought the chemical philosophy back to England. Close relations between chemical medicine and political and religious radicalism continued throughout our period. 'It is difficult for the modern reader to appreciate the intensity of the enthusiasm for chemistry' felt among the generation of 1640–60, Charles Webster tells us. 'His belief that chemical experiments were the key to the innermost secrets of nature inspired the practitioner to approach this labour with religious dedication'; and Webster quotes Robert Boyle (*The Great Instauration*, page 388).

But the point to stress is that in this period we cannot separate science from magic in the way that we do today. William Harvey, discoverer of the circulation of the blood, used to prescribe a medicine to be taken 'every new full moon'. Sir Francis Bacon, Sir Kenelm Digby and many other Fellows of the Royal Society believed in sympathetic magic – that a wound could be cured by applying a salve *to the weapon which caused it*. 'In those dark times', wrote John Aubrey of the days before the Civil War, 'astrologer, mathematician and conjuror were accounted the same things'. The first Duke of Buckingham, favourite of James I and Charles I, had his own astrologer, Dr Lambe. Rational politicians like John Lambert, Richard Overton, Bulstrode Whitelocke and Anthony Ashley-Cooper, first Earl of Shaftesbury, sought astrological advice. The Puritan divine John Preston took astrology seriously; the Ranter Laurence Clarkson and Elias Ashmole, FRS, practised it. In 1667 the second Duke of Buckingham was accused of high treason because he had caused the King's horoscope to be cast: his astrologer was tortured. (You will meet Ashley-Cooper and the second Duke of Buckingham later as Achitophel and Zimri respectively in Dryden's *Absalom and Achitophel;* Anthology, extract 134). There was a Society of Astrologers in London more than a decade before there was a Royal Society. One consequence of the liberation of the press in the sixteen-forties was that astrological books and especially astrological almanacs sold in vastly increased numbers: they were alleged by many contemporaries to have done more harm to the Royal cause than any other form of propaganda.

It is only from our modern vantage point – perhaps a temporary one – that we can separate what was 'rational' in seventeenth-century science from what was not. We must not allow the wisdom of hindsight to make us condescending about beliefs held by men like Harvey, Bacon, Boyle and Newton. Keith Thomas has suggested that astrologers were feeling their way towards a social science, a science of man in society. We know today that no science of astrology, alchemy or natural magic was to appear. But this outcome was not clear until the very end of our period. Isaac Newton said he first turned to the study of mathematics in order to understand a book on astrology (Manuel, page 81). He remained interested in alchemy (and in the study of Biblical prophecies) throughout the creative period of his life. 'The last of the magicians', Lord Keynes perceptively called him.

In the long run the influence of Protestantism worked against magic of all kinds, white as well as black, against charms, incantations, love potions. Countless Protestant sermons denouncing the miraculous transsubstantiation of bread and wine into body and blood may have helped to produce a materialist and sceptical attitude: miracles generally were pushed back into the epoch of the primitive church, and this greatly facilitated the task of expelling magic from everyday life. But this was true only in the very long run, for most men and women. One short-term consequence of the Reformation, Keith Thomas tells us, was that 'cunning men' (white witches) took over many jobs previously done by Roman Catholic priests. And the radical lower-class religious tradition was more interested in magic than intellectual Calvinism was. Radical heretics had many enemies in common with the scientists. Robert Browne, for instance, the father of Brownism (Congregationalism) criticized the scholastic logic of the universities because it was all 'in names and words, without any use'.

Against authority

The facts outlined above may suggest an analogy with Tawney's view of the connection of Protestantism and the rise of capitalism (see page 39 above). Modern science, like Protestantism, affected fundamental assumptions of traditional orthodoxy – the authority of Aristotle, Galen, Ptolemy in the one case, of the Fathers and of the church in the other. Scientists checked truth by experiment, and by their interpretation of the book of nature, Protestants by the experience of their hearts and by their interpretation of the Bible. William Harvey claimed to study anatomy 'not from books but from dissections, not from the positions of philosophers but from the fabric of nature'. The Puritan divine Thomas Taylor said almost the same thing: 'True knowledge of Christ is experimental'; it is acquired 'not . . . by reading, not out of books or relations, as the physician knows the virtue of books by reading; but by experience of himself'. Things were more important than the words used to describe them: on this Bacon and Puritans agreed. Intellectual exercises divorced from practice were as useless as truths learned by rote. Precedents must be checked by reason, but reasoning itself was subject to the test of experiment, of experience. George Hakewill, defending the Moderns against Goodman, appealed to evidence against the bishop's 'logic rule', to experience against authority.

The essence of Protestantism lies in its protest against blind authority, its reference of the test of truth ultimately to the individual conscience. This emphasis may have been important in creating an environment in which science could flourish. Rejection of clerical domination could very soon pass into erastianism and secularism, as it did in the Netherlands and England after their respective revolutions. It was this later phase of Protestantism which coincided with the rise of science, and perhaps conduced to it. Those Protestant states in which clerical domination was maintained – Geneva, Scotland – were late in making their contribution to science. The collapse of the church hierarchy in England in the early sixteen-forties ushered in two decades of liberty of speculation which enormously helped the rise and diffusion of scientific ideas (see pages 49–51 below).

Craftsmen, science and Protestantism

So perhaps we can see both Protestantism and the scientific revolution as deriving from changes in society. The early popularizers of science, Bacon in particular, advised natural philosophers to relate what they learned from scholarly books and classical authorities to the practice of craftsmen. Workshops and distilleries were the nearest most seventeenth-century experimentalists could get to a laboratory. Sprat said that 'the true natural philosophy should be principally intended' for 'mechanics and artisans'. The godly artisan was the man to whom Puritan preachers had always very specially directed their appeal.

In the eighty years before 1640 England, from being a backward country in science, became one of the most advanced. Gilbert's *De Magnete* (1600) summed up a great deal of experimental work done by English craftsmen, and put forward astronomical ideas which point towards the later concept of gravitational force. Thomas Hariot was using telescopes of his own manufacture to observe the stars at about the same time as Galileo announced his discoveries. The young Jeremiah Horrocks, entirely self-taught in astronomy, was one of the only two men in the world, so far as we know, to observe the transit of Venus in 1639. He was a Lancashire Puritan, who had been educated at the Puritan Emmanuel College, Cambridge. English mathematicians like Thomas Hariot and Edward Wright proved better at solving the problems of 'Mercator's projection' than Mercator himself. William Harvey's demonstration of the circulation of the blood in 1628 was a landmark. British botany was almost the best in Europe. Perhaps most important of all, no other European country, with the possible exception of Italy, had so high a proportion of scientific books *in the vernacular* as England. This last was the relevant point. It was not in the Latin-speaking academies of Oxford and Cambridge that modern science developed in England. Even when the scientists had been educated at a university, they normally had to leave it if they wanted to devote themselves to a scientific career, to join with the mechanic practitioners.

EXERCISE

So to sum up so far I would like you to consider in what ways Protestantism seemed to contribute to the scientific revolution in England, and what problems are raised by the attempt to see Protestantism as a causal factor?

DISCUSSION

Most of the points on both sides have been made, I think. I suggested that the existence of Calvinist churches in Hungary and Scotland did not lead to either capitalism or scientific developments there; Geneva is hardly a scientific centre at this period either. From the eighteenth century both capitalism and science begin to appear in Scotland, and science in Geneva, but by then the church had lost much of its authority in Scotland and Geneva, and the Union of England and Scotland in 1707 was surely at least as important in stimulating the rise of capitalism and science as Scotland's residual Calvinism.

Just as Tawney stressed that Protestant theology adapts more easily than Catholic to a capitalist society, so Merton stressed economic as well as ideological factors in the rise of modern science. What is perhaps most important is Protestantism's critical attitude towards authority, its emphasis on individual conscience and judgement ('the priesthood of all believers'), its tendency to play down the 'magical' element in religion, and the fact that in most states where Protestant churches were established this was accompanied by a relaxation of clerical control.

Puritanism and science

So far I have spoken about Protestantism. How about Puritanism? First we must define our terms. Unlike Charles Webster, whom I shall often be quoting, I prefer to keep the word 'Puritan' mainly for the period before 1640, and then to use it for those who wanted to remain within the Church of England but to push it further forward in a radical-Protestant direction, away from popery (see Block 1). So I distinguish not between 'Puritans' and 'Anglicans', but between 'Puritans' and 'Laudians'; all 'Puritans' were Anglicans though not all Anglicans were 'Puritans'. Only after 1660 is a distinction between nonconformists and Anglicans legitimate. As we saw in Block 3, before 1640 there was a third group of middle-of-the-road Calvinists, including Archbishops Grindal, Whitgift and Abbott, and bishops like Morton, Davenant and Joseph Hall, who disagreed with Puritans on organizational and disciplinary matters, but shared their predestinarian theology. Bacon must have counted such men as 'Puritans' when in 1624 he said that men so called formed 'the greatest body of the subjects' (see Tyacke in the Reader, article 12). Certainly, if we are considering the implications for science, Calvinists of all kinds ought to be counted together against Catholics and Laudians.

So for the period before 1640 I see no very significant distinction between Calvinist Anglicans and Puritans. Nor do I see Laudian Anglicans as hostile to science, in the way that Counter-Reformation Catholicism perhaps was. The important fact is the establishment in England of a state-controlled church with a theology which was predominantly Calvinist until the rise of Laud. Because the Laudians were totally dependent on Royal favour they never succeeded in establishing clerical control over society, though many MPs feared that that was their aim.

After 1640 we can continue to use the word 'Puritan' and we can think of Puritanism as the ideology of the leading activists among the Parliamentarians; but once the Laudian establishment collapsed, divisions among 'Puritans' soon revealed themselves (see pages 50–1 below).

New possibilities

It was Thomas Hobbes who noted the importance of change as an intellectual stimulus, 'it being almost all one for a man to be always sensible of the same things, and not to be sensible of anything'. This intellectual stimulus came from the economic developments and the political revolutions of the period, as well as from Protestantism. Your Reader contains Joan Thirsk's description of the new industries which were springing up in England in the early seventeenth century (article 6). This and the experience of long-distance overseas trade, and the beginnings of colonization, must have given men a new confidence in the possibility of controlling the world they lived in.

The sixteenth and seventeenth centuries were a period in which an increasing proportion of the population became conscious of the possibility of eliminating scarcity. Throughout history famine and starvation had dogged humanity. The traditional ruling class had no need to bother about scarcity: whoever else starved, its members always had enough. The poorest peasantry and wage-labourers had no other perspective than intermittent starvation. The arbitrary ways of God could therefore seem as incomprehensible as the weather, upon which the harvest depended. But from at least the sixteenth century some merchants, yeomen and artisans found that they could lift themselves into relative abundance by a combination of hard work and good luck. Puritanism found many of its adherents among these social groups, lumped together by contemporaries as 'the middling sort'.

Protestantism contributed by emphasizing the duty of working hard in one's calling. But even individual escape from poverty involved tremendous effort and concentration. It might also involve breaches of what was customarily regarded as correct behaviour. Men who had to follow new courses had to have an inner certainty and confidence. Theories of predestination suggest not only the colossal power of the blind forces which seemed to dominate society but also the possibility of liberation for the lucky few. By intensive study of the Bible (and especially its prophecies) men could understand destiny and become free. Some may even have conceived of the possibility of total escape from the curse of scarcity, from the burden which had rested on humanity's back from the beginning of history.

'The Lord was with Joseph, and he was a lucky fellow': Tawney has made these words from Tyndale's sixteenth-century translation of the Bible famous. The successes of sixteenth and seventeenth century trade, industry and science confirmed and justified this new confidence. Slowly nature came to be thought of as a machine that could be understood, controlled and improved upon by knowledge. It is one thing to dominate nature through command of serfs and cattle, as the ruling class had done from time immemorial; it is something quite different to invent machines for the same purpose. The potentialities of cattle and serfs are limited; the potentialities of machines handled by free men are limitless. Bacon once said that all sciences could be perfected in a few years; Sir William Petty believed that 'the impediments to England's greatness are but contingent and removable'. We can see how this would help to make 'the mechanization of the world picture' acceptable.

In the seventeenth century man's age-old helplessness in the face of hostile nature was being broken down; ordinary men (as opposed to lords of serfs) could begin to envisage the possibility of controlling their environment, including the social and political institutions under which they lived, and even of eliminating scarcity. Calvinism aided science by removing mystery and pantheistic overtones from nature, by its emphasis on law, and its insistence on co-operation with God's purposes. For in order to co-operate with God's purposes one must first understand them: the more historical and scientific knowledge one possessed, the more capable one was of *active* co-operation. Science was for action, not contemplation: here Bacon, Hakewill, Wilkins were at one with the Calvinist theologians. The scientific approach to God's works in the universe was one way of getting to know him. The world glorifies God because of what it is: God himself pronounced it good. Hence the importance of studying it scientifically so as to read its lessons right.

'Knowledge without practice is no knowledge', wrote the Puritan author of the marginal headings to Richard Greenham's *Works*. In 1648 John Wilkins wrote, 'Our best and most divine knowledge is intended for action'; 'Those may justly be accounted barren studies which do not conduce to practice as their proper end'. Similarly, the Puritan Thomas Taylor said: 'We teach that only doers shall be saved, and by their doing though not for their doing . . . The profession of religion is no such gentlemanlike life or trade, whose rents come in by their stewards, whether they sleep or wake, work or play'. Christians must often look into their debt books and cast up their reckonings; 'but a bankrupt has not heart to this business'. Bacon transferred this spirit to science when he said 'Not to try is a greater risk than to fail'. 'The improvement of man's mind and the improvement of his lot are one and the same thing.'

Bacon reminds us of Milton's *Areopagitica* when he writes 'It is reserved only for God and angels to be lookers-on'. Bacon was criticizing Aristotle's preference for the contemplative over the active life. Milton refused to praise a 'fugitive and cloistered virtue' that held men back from political struggle. 'The soul of religion is the practical part', said Bunyan, who expected God to ask at Doomsday, 'Were you doers or talkers only?' Here we are at the root of Calvinism's contribution to science as well as to the Parliamentary cause. John Dury wrote that 'What art or science soever doth not advantage man-kind, either to bring him nearer unto God in his soul, or to free him from the bondage of corruption in his body, is not at all to be entertained: because at the best it is but a diversion of the mind'. Part of God's covenant, Hakewill thought, is the orderly and perpetual working of the universe; or, as the Puritan John Preston put it, 'God alters no law of nature'. 'Theology', Charles Webster rightly insists, 'must be accepted as a factor directly relevant to the formation of scientific concepts' (*The Great Instauration*, pages 493–4). The great political and scientific advances of the seventeenth century owed much to Calvinist thought. Calvinism's main achievements, it may be para-doxically suggested, were in the last analysis this-worldly.

'Bacon's philosophy', Webster tells us, 'seemed to be providentially designed for the needs of the Puritan Revolution'. (Charles Webster uses this phrase for what we in this course have normally called the English Revolu-tion.) 'Indeed, this suitability was not accidental, considering that the philosopher had an intellectual ancestry largely in common with the English Puritans.' (This does not mean of course that Bacon sympathized with their political programme: he wanted to preserve national unity and bring about change through the monarchy.)

> Bacon gave precise and systematic philosophical expression to the anti-authoritarianism, inductivism and utilitarianism which were such important factors in the puritan scale of values . . .
>
> The Puritans were conditioned by the ideal of a dedicated voca-tional life, which involved the most efficient use of abilities for per-sonal advantage and public service. The glorification of God was thus linked to the idea of the most efficient exploitation of human and material resources. In line with this ethical perspective we find among the Puritans a general dissatisfaction with previous standards, receptivity to alternatives, enthusiasm for efficient education and vocational training, and a ceaseless search for general improve-ment . . . The patient and accurate methods of experimental science, penetrating slowly towards an understanding of the secondary causes of things in the search for a gradual reconquest of nature, represented the form of intellectual and practical endeavour most suited to the puritan mentality . . . Every step brought further insight into the providence of God, so constantly reaffirming the correctness of the procedure.
>
> (*The Great Instauration*, pages 514, 505–6.)

Webster suggests that 'Bacon's ideas about the Fall [of Man] . . . and the moral conditions for restoration, were completely in keeping with the dominant Calvinist tradition in England' (page 329). 'Man by the Fall', Bacon wrote, 'fell at the same time from his state of innocency and from his dominion over created things. Both these losses can even in this life be partially repaired; the former by religion and faith, the latter by arts and sciences'. By the exercise of reason and by intense effort a new society could be built on earth which would recreate the abundance of Eden and eliminate much if not all of human sinfulness. Labour, the curse of fallen man, might be the means for him to rise again. Such ideas look forward to Milton, and indeed to Gerrard Winstanley.

Bacon had a millenarian vision which fitted very well with Puritanism. The first draft of his philosophic programme included the prophecy of Daniel. 'Many shall pass to and fro, and science shall be increased'. Charles Webster sums up:

> The Puritan Revolution was . . . seen as a period of promise, when God would allow science to become the means to bring about a new paradise on earth. Science accordingly assumed considerable significance in the puritan programme and the puritan intellectuals became committed to a dedicated attempt to procure the return of man's dominion over nature . . . The revolutionaries felt that they were in a position to reap the reward of a national greatness based on the revival of learning, which had been spurned by the corrupt Stuart kings . . . [This belief] initially dependent on millenarian eschatology, could persist as millenarianism gradually waned in significance during the later part of the century, and became transmuted into a general secular belief in progress, of the kind which is found during the Enlightenment.
>
> (Charles Webster, *The Great Instauration*, pages xvi, 514, 507; see also my discussion of millenarianism, page 32 above.)

It was only after 1640 that Bacon's reputation and influence acquired the supremacy they were never to lose. More of Bacon's works were published in England in 1640–1 than in all the fourteen years after his death in 1626, including *The Advancement of Learning* (1640); *New Atlantis* was published in 1643. Bacon was popularized especially in the writings of John Wilkins and by Samuel Hartlib (see below for Hartlib). The liberty of the press in the revolutionary decades also helped Hakewill to get to a much larger audience, and enabled Harvey's works, originally written in Latin, to be disseminated in the vernacular.

After the Restoration, Henry Stubbe tried to blame Bacon for the English Revolution. Bacon, he said, had been responsible for inculcating 'contempt of the ancient ecclesiastical and civil jurisdiction and the old government as well as the governors of the realm'. Certainly the radical Puritans included some of the most enthusiastic Baconians. Such men took over Bacon's belief that it was possible to liberate mankind on earth from the consequences of the Fall of Man.

The Revolution

After 1640 clerical control broke down generally. In the breakthrough of free discussion in the next two decades all possible heresies were discussed: most of them had political implications. Milton and Henry Parker suggested that the Bible was to be interpreted with one eye on the earthly welfare of men and women. The most conspicuous proponent of Baconian reform was Samuel Hartlib, disciple of the great Bohemian educational reformer Comenius. For Hartlib, as for Bacon, to endow the condition and life of man with new powers and works was a religious duty. Bacon's proclaimed object had been 'to establish and extend the power and dominion of the human race itself over the universe'. It was in this spirit that Robert Boyle's Invisible College in the sixteen-forties practised 'so extensive a charity that it reaches unto everything called man'. It is not surprising that the radical Puritan Hugh Peter in 1646 told Parliament that it should further 'the new experimental philosophy', or that Milton was a Baconian. Hartlib used the freedom of the revolutionary decades to popularize a programme of social, economic, religious, educational and scientific reform. He greatly influenced men like Boyle, Petty and Henry Oldenburg, later Secretary of the Royal Society. Under Hartlib's influence, would-be reformers of Oxford and Cambridge like John Hall, Noah Biggs and John Webster called for more anatomy and chemistry to be studied in the universities, as well as alchemy, astrology and natural magic (see Anthology, extracts 107–10; and Block 4, 'Education in England to 1660').

Charles Webster has pointed out that 'advocates of the new philosophy were extremely successful in recommending themselves to the new men who assumed power during the Puritan Revolution . . . Consequently there was a marked elevation of science and medicine in the public esteem and an acceleration in the pace of scientific development'. 'It is doubtful whether at any other time in English history scientific intellectuals have assumed such importance in national administration' (The Great Instauration, pages 84, 519).

There was general agreement among contemporaries about the scientific advances made in the sixteen-forties and fifties. Marchamont Nedham, himself a medical man, thought that more progress had been made in the profession of medicine since 1640 'than ever was done in the world before'. The Royalist Walter Charleton spoke in 1657 of great advances in natural philosophy, medicine, optics, astronomy, geometry and chemistry by men 'now living in England and as yet in the prime of their strength and years'. Both Aubrey and Sir William Temple dated the end of belief in 'fairies, sprites, witchcraft and enchantments' to these decades. 'All before 1650 is ancient', says the historian of technology, Charles Singer; 'all after modern'.

In the short run the effect of the Revolution was to strengthen the influence of the Paracelsians. More Paracelsian books were published in England in the sixteen-fifties than in the whole preceding century, and there was a great flood of medical literature in the vernacular. 'The cheap and simple Paracelsian remedies', Charles Webster remarks, 'appeared to offer a means of relieving the medical problems of the growing population of the poor' (page 288). At Oxford by the sixteen-fifties the ideas of Van Helmont and Harvey became dominant; Webster sees a 'revolutionary change' between the medical ideology prevailing in the Laudian period and that of the sixteen-fifties. For the first time there were effective teaching and research medical schools in English universities, medical text-books became at least as good as those on the continent; the foundations were laid for the development of teaching hospitals, and there were proposals for the medical care of the poor (Webster, pages 138–43). The new fashion took institutional form in the College of Graduate Physicians, sponsored by Hartlib's disciple William Rand, which aspired to break the monopoly of the College of Physicians. But the College of Physicians itself, under Harvey's guidance, responded to the spirit of the time by modernizing its ways so as to incorporate a great deal of chemical medicine.

Yet the free-for-all of speculation went much too far for the orthodox in these decades – including 'excesses' in science as well as in other spheres. Richard Overton, the Leveller, suggested a scientific experiment to test the immortality of the soul; the Quakers George Fox and Edward Burrough called for a laboratory analysis to see whether bread and wine could really be transformed into body and blood. William Walwyn and Gerrard Winstanley explained religious experience in psycho-physical terms; excessive fasting might lead to visions and ecstasies. Boyle and many early Fellows of the Royal Society felt it to be the job of science to refute such materialism (see 'The Breakdown of Calvinism', page 33, and Jacob, article 19 in the Reader).

Newton's later insistence that the universe was not eternal was part of a conscious assertion of divine providence against 'atheists', whether radical or Hobbist. Even when Joseph Glanvill, Fellow of the Royal Society, was defending the superiority of the Moderns, he felt it necessary to add, 'I intend not the former discourse in favour of any new-broach'd conceit in divinity' (Anthology, extract 136). Many of the scientific radicals had also been involved in schemes for religious, social or political reform. Sir William Temple 'always looked upon alchemy in natural philosophy to be like enthusiasm in divinity, and to have troubled the world much to the same purpose'.

The Restoration

After 1660 everything connected with radicalism was rejected by those who were in a position to influence public opinion. 'Enthusiasm', prophecy and astrology as a rival system of explanation to Christianity, were all out of favour. The College of Graduate Physicians collapsed. Its successor in the sixties, the Society of Chemical Physicians, was unsuccessful in achieving the institutional status that the Royal Society had won, and was forced back upon the support of unlearned 'empirics'. The College of Physicians had embraced enough chemical medicine to be able to ward off their rivals. The latter were then dismissed as 'fanatics in physic, supporters of the late rebellion', who wanted to open medicine to 'hatters, cobblers and tinkers'. So society's verdicts become self-validating. Over and above its scientific merits, the mechanical philosophy came to be seen as the best defence against 'enthusiasm' and 'mechanic atheism'. Thomas Sprat claimed that it was the job of science and the Royal Society 'to shake off the shadows and to scatter the mists which fill the minds of men with a vain consternation'.

After the Restoration scientists felt that they had to organize themselves under official patronage if they were to survive. Many of the leading figures in the Royal Society had cooperated actively with the republican governments. But intensive lobbying at court won the support of influential patrons, and ultimately that of Charles II himself, who wisely became head of the Royal Society as well as of the Church of England. Any peer who wished might be elected a Fellow of the Society; the Fellows actively associated themselves with propaganda against 'fanatics' and the radicals generally. They survived the hostility of Oxford and Cambridge; by 1665 the Secretary of the Royal Society was even hoping 'to insinuate the designs of the Society' into Oxford.

The Royal Society was more eclectic than historians used to think when they took Sprat's propagandist *History of the Royal Society* at its face value. (See T. Hoppen in the Reader, article 18.) The Fellows were not all believers in the mechanical philosophy, nor did they all accept a single type of Baconianism. Some of the *best* seventeenth-century scientists still accepted bodies of ideas which would today be regarded as irrational. And the lines between what we regard as scientific and unscientific were crossed. John Webster, an early critic, on scientific grounds, of belief in witchcraft, was a Hermeticist; Joseph Glanvill, critic of Hermeticism on scientific grounds and defender of the Royal Society, also defended belief in witches. John Dryden, FRS, believed in astrology; Dr John Locke, FRS, believed that kidney pains could be cured by burying a sample of the patient's urine in a stone jar.

The Royal Society tried hard to cover up its roots in the English Revolution, and its propaganda deceived some historians. Charles Webster sees more clearly:

> The puritan movement which collapsed so completely in 1660 as an ecclesiastical and political force, exercised an enduring effect in the areas of science, technology and agriculture. It would have been injudicious for contemporaries to admit such continuity, and indeed they were obliged to distract attention from it, but the marks of

puritanism were indelibly stamped into the fabric of restoration science... Taken as a whole, the scientific literature of the Puritan Revolution helped to create a climate of opinion favourable to the philosophical programme of the early Royal Society... It became almost impossible to suppress the fertile developments in popular medicine which had occurred in the two decades of de-restriction.

(*The Great Instauration*, pages 516, 491 and 308.)

In England after 1660 'Puritans' were forced to choose between conformity to a politically weakened Church of England on the one hand, and the provincial and limited world of dissent on the other. As Webster put it, after the Restoration the natural sciences and experimental philosophy 'became an established feature of English higher education, but only for the nonconformist followers of the puritan reformers' (page 244). Science was more useful to the economy than dissent, and so the Royal Society institutionalized itself under Royal patronage. It was a mixed blessing. The gentleman amateur Fellows of the Society were interested either in utilitarian tips for agriculture, or in monstrous births and other exciting phenomena, or in watching conjuring-trick type experiments. Newton's *Principia* was approved for publication by Samuel Pepys, then President of the Royal Society. Pepys was no scientist: he had painfully learnt his multiplication table at the age of thirty. He was President of a gentlemen's club. The Industrial Revolution of the eighteenth century owed little to the Royal Society; inventors were very often nonconformists, educated in dissenting academies. More important, the Royal Society did not take up the schemes for equality of educational opportunity which many scientists had supported during the revolutionary decades. So the reservoir of scientific talent in the lower classes which these schemes had envisaged remained untapped, and 'England advanced towards the technological age with a population ill-equipped to take the fullest advantage of its resources'. The words are Charles Webster's again (quoted in *The World Turned Upside Down*, page 305): they throw light perhaps on some of the subsequent weaknesses of the British economy.

Conclusion

This historical background may help us to find our way through controversies about Protestantism, Puritanism and science. It is, as I have suggested, largely a matter of definition. After 1640 the traditional Church of England collapsed, and 'Puritans' evolved into different denominations. Radical sects, like Baptists, Quakers and Muggletonians, organized themselves in far greater numbers than the congregations which had existed before 1640; Presbyterians differentiated themselves more clearly from Independents (as well as from sectaries), though both Presbyterians and Independents remained within the Cromwellian state church – as did most middle-of-the-road Calvinists. After 1660 the radical sects were excluded from the Church of England; some Presbyterians and Independents conformed, some excluded themselves. But the Church of England after 1660 was very different from the Laudian church of the thirties; the majority of those (or the descendants of those) who had been 'Puritans' before 1640 conformed after 1660. And this naturally applied particularly to scientists. Those whose concerns were primarily religious – including the scientist John Ray – left the Church of England after 1660. Newton conformed with some reservations. But many other scientists – Wilkins, Ward, Boyle, Petty – who had happily accepted the Cromwellian state church in the fifties, conformed to the restored episcopal church with equal complacency.

EXERCISE

How then should we begin to assess the relative contributions of Puritanism and the events of the English Revolution to the scientific revolution in England?

DISCUSSION

Our answer to this question depends largely on the definitions we use. When historians anxiously count Fellows of the Royal Society to decide whether 'Puritans' or 'non-Puritans' preponderated, they are playing a definitions game. 'To a large extent the conclusions reached have been determined by the procedures adopted', as Charles Webster rightly says (page 89). One scholar worked with a definition of 'Puritan' which would have excluded not only John Wilkins (that was his object) but also John Milton and Richard Baxter, who has been called 'the most representative Puritan in History': certainly Weber and Tawney treat him as such. Another assumed – with divine simplicity – that anyone who became a bishop after 1660 could not have been a Puritan in the forties or fifties; and that no one wishing to be charitable to all, or who was moderate, could possibly have been a Puritan. Another has a definition of 'Royalist' – as opposed to 'Puritan' – which includes Roger Boyle, the Marquis of Argyll (executed in 1661 as a traitor), and Sir Anthony Ashley-Cooper, Cromwell's right-hand man, later Dryden's 'false Achitophel'. However, this eccentricity was cancelled out by the even greater eccentricity of counting Major-General Monck and Henry Mordaunt as Parliamentarians. Monck got a dukedom and Mordaunt an earldom for their share in bringing about the restoration of Charles II. It is all a rather foolish game, which throws no more light on the origins of science in England than counting MPs throws light on the causes of the Civil War (see Block 3, 'Origins of the Civil War').

Professor Shapiro has argued, plausibly enough, that a majority of those Fellows of the Royal Society whose religious views can be ascertained became under Charles II what were called Latitudinarians. 'A Latitudinarian', said Bunyan, 'can, as to religion, turn and twist ... like the weathercock that stands on the steeple'. (The editor of your edition of *The Pilgrim's Progress* suggests that Mr Worldly Wiseman may be a Latitudinarian: note 2, page 375). One characteristic of Latitudinarians, which Bunyan no doubt had in mind, was that the leading figures among them had accepted the Cromwellian church, so most of them were in Merton's definition 'Puritans' or ex-Puritans. Thus all parties to the unreal dispute can be satisfied. Charles Webster, more sensibly, insists that since any gentleman could be elected a member of the social club which the Royal Society was, we should look rather at the nucleus of scientists who were active both in their profession and in the Society. This too produces a majority of ex-Puritans or Latitudinarians (*The Great Instauration*, page 91; see also J. R. Jacob, page 172, and *C of R*, pages 208–9, 252–3).

J. R. Jacob carried the argument a stage further. 'Boyle's puritanism, produced by revolution, is no longer [after 1660] puritanism as Merton defined it'. Boyle's views changed 'under the impact of events', which frightened orthodox Puritans no less than traditional Laudians and middle-of-the-road Calvinists. First he rejected the traditional aristocratic ethic. But then he felt that orthodox religion had to be defended: his 'corpuscularian' philosophy was consciously evolved in controversy with radical sectarians, with mortalists whom Boyle believed to be no better than atheists. The study of nature, Boyle concluded and the Royal Society proclaimed, is the best defence against 'mechanic atheism' (J. R. Jacob, pages 85–7, 107, 114, 127–8, 172).

Whatever we decide about Puritanism and the scientific revolution, there can be little doubt about the impact of the English Revolution upon science. Merton established that 'an unusually large number of persons who later made their mark in these fields turned to science and technology in the sixteen-forties and fifties'. This applies, Webster adds, 'to almost all the "active nucleus" of the Royal Society, and to the vast majority of the "active members" ... Of the slightly older generation, very many had been educated in a predominantly puritan environment before 1640' (page 42). Wilkins, Petty, Wallis, Oldenburg and Boyle all spent their formative years during the Revolution, and 'all were undoubtedly centrally involved in the political and religious affairs of the dominant party during that period'. Wilkins and Wallis, in particular, 'were from the outset regarded by the parliamentary authorities as persons of unswerving loyalty'.

> Puritanism and the period of the Puritan Revolution are more important for the understanding of developments after 1660 than is generally conceded ... The rise of experimental science correlates almost exactly with the upsurge of puritanism ... There is ample evidence to suggest that the entire puritan movement was conspicuous in its cultivation of the sciences, that its members became vigorous proponents of a variety of new approaches to natural philosophy, and that ...their scientific beliefs were framed with conscious reference to their religious views.
>
> (*The Great Instauration*, pages 496–503.)

So perhaps the question which has caused so much discussion, 'What did Puritanism contribute to the rise of science?' is wrongly posed. Perhaps I posed it wrongly in *C of R*. Puritanism and science both thrived in a society where clerical domination had been reduced, and in which economic activity was bustling. Both developed rapidly in periods of intellectual liberty and discussion. The contribution of Protestantism to the rise of science has I think been established. But Protestantism is much wider than Puritanism. Church of England Calvinists who later turned into Latitudinarians, on the one hand, and radical sectaries on the other, both contributed to the rise of modern science, though in very different ways. But if we see Puritanism as an important contributory factor to the English Revolution, then its indirect connection with the rise of science is great: for the English Revolution, as I think Charles Webster has conclusively shown, created conditions in which science blossomed faster and more freely than it would have done had there been no Revolution.

One last point. Sprat's *History of the Royal Society* propagandized on behalf of plain prose, written in 'the language of artisans, countrymen and merchants'. (Discussed in *The Development of Prose.*) For our purposes it is relevant to emphasize that this is an inheritance from the Puritan preachers, who opposed the florid, 'witty' sermon-style favoured by preachers at the courts of James I and Charles I, and insisted on a straightforward prose capable of convincing ordinary men, particularly godly artisans. John Wilkins summed up this tradition in his *Ecclesiastes or, a Discourse Concerning the Gift of Preaching* (1646) and *A Discourse Concerning the Gift of Prayer* (1651). The title-page of the former work reproduced almost word for word a paragraph on preaching from the Directory produced by the Presbyterian Westminster Assembly of Divines; its Preface referred approvingly to Parliament's purge of 'scandalous ministers' – both hall-marks of a Puritan. The development of pamphlet warfare in the forties and fifties increased the importance of appealing to the literate 'middling sort'. Sprat naturally did not mention either this or the Puritan tradition when he made his programmatic statement. But it is clear that in this field too both Puritanism and the English Revolution exercised a significant influence.

References

R. K. Merton (1938) 'Science, Technology and Society in Seventeenth-Century England' *Osiris*, IV.

C. Webster (1975) *The Great Instauration: Science, Medicine and Reform, 1626–1660*, Duckworth.

C. Hill (1975) *The World Turned Upside Down*, Penguin.

M.C. Jacob (1976) *The Newtonians and the English Revolution, 1689–1720*, Harvester Press.

J. R. Jacob (1977) *Robert Boyle and the English Revolution*, New York.

B. J. Shapiro (1968) 'Latitudinarianism and Science in Seventeenth-Century England', *Past and Present*, No. 40.

R. H. Tawney (1938) *Religion and the Rise of Capitalism*, Penguin.

F. Manuel (1980) *A Portrait of Sir Isaac Newton*, Muller.

Music: The Commonwealth

Contents

Music: The Commonwealth

1 Introduction

The social and political changes taking place during the sixteen-fifties (and, incidentally, I will here be dealing with the sixteen-forties as well) could hardly help affecting music, although evidence of this is not always explicit. Indeed, in art music there were few direct references to the events of the period. 'A Sad Pavan for these Distracted Times' by Thomas Tomkins (1572–1656), written a fortnight after the execution of Charles I, is one of the few examples – you can hear it on record 1 (Seventeenth-century England: Music 1, OU 69, side 2, band 1. However, references to current events are much more frequent in the broadside ballads. At first many of these were sympathetic to the Parliament but during the sixteen-forties the King became increasingly popular. 'Hey, Then Up Go We' (1642) gets the best of both worlds by posing as a Parliamentarian song although its inclusion in *Loyal Songs Written Against the Rump Parliament* points to its Royalist sympathies and that its intention was satirical. The music can be found on record 1, side 2, band 2. The tune is 'Cuckolds All A-Row' (see Block 2, 'Music: Before the Civil War', page 65). Here's an abridged version of the text (several verses are omitted):

> Know this, my brethren, Heav'n is clear,
>   And all the clouds are gone,
> The righteous man shall flourish now;
>   Good days are coming on.
> Then come, my brethren, and be glad,
>   And eke rejoice with me;
> Lawn sleeves and Rochets[1] shall go down,
>   And hey, then up go we.
>
> Whate'er the Popish hands have built,
>   Our hammers shall undo,
> We'll break their pipes, and burn their copes,
>   And pull down churches too;
> We'll exercise within the groves,
>   And teach beneath a tree,
> We'll make a pulpit of a cask,
>   And hey, then up go we.
>
> The name of lords shall be abhorr'd
>   For every man's a brother,
> No reason why in church and state
>   One man should rule another;
> But when the change of government
>   Shall set our fingers free,
> We'll make these wanton sisters stoop,
>   And hey, then up go we.
>
> What though the King and Parliament
>   Do not accord together,
> We have more cause to be content,
>   This is our sunshine weather;
> For if that reason should take place,
>   And they should once agree,
> Who would be in a Roundhead's case,
>   For hey, then up go we.

[1]Bishops.

EXERCISE

What actions and ideas associated with the Puritans is the writer satirizing?

DISCUSSION

1 The abolition of bishops.

2 The Puritan opposition to popish practices.

3 Preaching by the laity and the radical attack upon the institutions of the church in general.

4 The equality of men in church and state.

The final verse turns the tables and reveals the satire!

Another Royalist ballad actually featured the King as a protagonist, as well as Cromwell and the populace – 'A Coffin for King Charles; A Crown for Cromwell; A Pit for the People' (1649) – yet easily the most famous ballad of the time was Martin Parker's 'When the King Enjoys His own Again' (1643). Despite the King's death (or because of it), this ballad became increasingly popular during the Commonwealth until it earned the reputation of actually promoting the Restoration itself!

A survey of the ballads produced during the Commonwealth reveals that in general there was little change in the types of ballads written. The range of subject matter was as wide as before. Listen to 'The Two Jeering Lovers' (1656) on record 1, side 2, band 3 (to the tune 'Bonny sweet Robin'). This consists of a dialogue between 'Dick Downright of the Country, and pretty witty Nancy of the City'. The ballad tells of their 'wooing, winning and wedding', in a very light-hearted way.

Many ballads contained pro-Royalist sentiments and this partly reflected the political bias of the ballad writers themselves. Also the various measures taken against the ballad writers by Parliament were hardly likely to call forth goodwill. Cromwell himself suffered considerably at their hands. They heaped abuse on him for reasons ranging from his pretension to the crown to his red nose. However, in 'Joyful News for England', he is favourably regarded, at least by implication. The ballad writer reports on the peace settlement concluded between England and Holland on 6 April 1654 and basks in the new power and prestige bestowed upon his native land which resulted.

> The Noble States of Holland,
>   Embassadors have sent,
> To England's Lord Protector,
>   Worse dangers to prevent
> To have a Peace concluded,
>   To which he did agree,
> That bloody wars twixt them and us,
>   Forth-with should ceased be:
> This is the bravest News indeed,
>   That e'er to England came,
> The Dutchmen will be friends with us,
>   and we will be the same.
>
> Also from other Countries
>   the Messengers do hie,
> Both France and many Nations more,
>   with England do comply:
> For fear of disagreement,
>   what after might befall,
> Thus Englishmen from East to West
>   are fear'd and lov'd of all,

This is the Noblest News indeed,
      that e'er to England came,
The Hollanders are friends with us,
      and we are friends with them.

2 Changes

The reference in the second verse of 'Hey, Then Up Go We' to 'pipes' is not to tobacco pipes but to organ pipes. As you will hear in Radio Programme 8, *Puritans and Church Music*, the Puritans objected to elaborate music in church and some organs were destroyed by over-hasty soldiers before an official ordinance was passed to have them dismantled and removed. The cathedral and church choirs were disbanded.

Court patronage, as well as church patronage, came to an end. The King's Music and the Chapel Royal were disbanded, and, considering the large number and distinction of the musicians involved, this would appear to have been a hard blow to the profession. However, many of these musicians, because of their high reputations, soon found pupils and continued to earn their living by teaching. Naturally enough, those who were well-known Royalists – Henry Lawes dedicated his *Choice Psalms* to the King in 1648 – were deeply shocked by his death and feared that they might be arrested by the Parliamentarians. But this did not happen.

The fate of individual musicians varied. Tomkins, at the age of seventy-three, was forced to retire from his post as organist at Worcester Cathedral following the second siege of the town in 1646. William Child (1606–97), appointed one of the organists at St George's Chapel, Windsor in 1632, and well-liked by Charles I, also retired and took up farming. Several composers joined Royalist forces, including Henry Cooke (d. 1672) and William Lawes. The latter lost his life at the siege of Chester (1645) and was personally mourned by the King.

Other musicians transferred their allegiance from one side to the other as needs be. Davis Mell (1604–62), although once a court violinist under Charles I, could describe himself in a petition to Cromwell as 'Gentleman of His Highness Musique' (i.e. Cromwell's) and was present at the Protector's funeral. During the Restoration, he was appointed a member of Charles II's band and its joint director! Some musicians seem to have been hardly affected at all, at least financially. For instance, Henry Loosemore, the organist at King's College, Cambridge, retained his post throughout the period and several of the musicians at Westminster Abbey continued to draw their salaries.

All in all, it was the singing-men in the cathedrals that suffered most during the Commonwealth, although their situation was alleviated to a certain extent by the creation of a relief scheme by Parliament. Another group of musicians, the freelance players in London, also suffered considerable hardship. Following the closure of the theatres in 1642, a tract, 'The Actor's Remonstrance or Complaint for the silencing of their Profession', was printed, which described how musicians in the theatres lost their jobs: Their 'music that was held so delectable and precious that they scorned to come to a tavern under twenty shillings salary for two hours, now wander with their instruments under their cloaks – I mean such as have any – into all houses of good fellowship, saluting every room where there is company with, *Will you have any music, gentlemen?*'

Developments

Despite the changes wrought in the lives of musicians by the shift in patronage from the court and church to the middle class, musical life continued to flourish, if not with an added intensity. There is considerable evidence to suggest that the waits carried out their duties during the period of Puritan control as before. Certainly at Yarmouth, Norwich and Newcastle this was so. Also music apprenticeships continued to be granted. Many Puritans were in fact keen musicians and to cater for the widening interest in music, music printing took on a new lease of life. In addition, a series of musical meetings also developed, which led, as we shall see (in 'Restoration Music' in Block 10, *A Culture Changed*) to the first public concerts.

Puritan music-lovers included Milton, Bunyan, Colonel Hutchinson and Whitelocke, and Cromwell himself was undoubtedly a musical connoisseur. He had his own small group of household musicians, which included Mell and the organist, John Hingston (d. 1683). Among Hingston's duties was to teach music to Cromwell's daughters. Cromwell requested that the organ Hingston had played at Magdalen College, Oxford should be moved to Hampton Court. Whereas its use at Magdalen was now prohibited, it *was* played at Hampton Court. Cromwell's musicians drew up a petition outlining the problems that musicians faced at the time, and suggested building a college of music in London where musicians could be educated. This was considered by a government committee but, possibly due to lack of funds, no action was taken.

Despite the ban on theatrical performances, stage works were produced during the Interregnum. Shirley's *The Contention of Ajax and Ulysses* (1653) and *Cupid and Death* (1653), both of which contain features derived from the masque, were given. In 1656 these were followed by the first English opera, *The Siege of Rhodes*. Sir William Davenant (1606–68), a Royalist knighted by Charles I, was able with the support of such Puritans as Whitelocke and John Maynard, the Solicitor-General, to promote what he called 'entertainments' with 'the Story sung in *Recitative* Music'. And these proved very popular. *The Siege of Rhodes* had several revivals. The music was composed, like that for the masques, by several collaborators, including Henry Lawes, Cooke and Matthew Locke (see Block 10, 'Restoration Music'). Unfortunately none of the music has survived.

The central figure in music printing was John Playford (1623–86). With shrewd business sense, he realized that the market for music publications was a potentially expanding one – as Roger North put it in *The Musical Grammarian*, 'many chose rather to fiddle at home than to go out and be knocked on the head abroad' – and proceeded both to provide and encourage this market with a wide range of publications. He began in 1650 with *The English Dancing Master* (actually dated 1651), a collection of popular tunes, with 'plain and easy rules' for dancing. This proved so popular that it was subsequently reissued many times. In the next year came *A Musical Banquet* in three parts, comprising lessons on the lyra viol*, a collection of dances, and a collection of catches* and rounds* followed in 1652 with *Select Ayres and Dialogues** (songs by Wilson, Henry Lawes, etc.). (Words with asterisks appear in the glossary on page 63.) Other publications during the sixteen-fifties included further collections of songs and catches, primers for different instruments, and an introduction to performing and composing music. Following the erratic publication of music during Charles I's reign, this was a positive wealth of publications (an almost six-fold increase).

An interesting point arises from the different editions of *The English Dancing Master*. An advertisement for the first edition states that the tunes are written for the treble viol. However, with the second edition of 1652, the tunes are for the violin. Also, in the 1658 edition of Playford's *Introduction to the Skill of Music* a section is devoted to 'Instructions for the Treble Violin . . . a cheerful and sprightly instrument, and much practised of late'. Here is evidence that the treble viol was becoming ousted by the violin, a process that was clearly well under way during the Commonwealth. Violins, the 'High-Priz'd Noise' of which was 'fit to make a Man's Ear Glow, and fill his brain full of frisks' (Thomas Mace, *Music's Monument*, 1676), had been used as early as Elizabeth's reign for playing dance music at court and had become increasingly popular during the first half of the seventeenth century. Remember that William Lawes's Fantasia from his First Suite was composed

for viols whereas the later Eighth Sonata used the violin (see Block 2, pages 64–5). During the latter half of the seventeenth century, the more piercing tone of the violin and its greater agility were more suitable for the nimble, 'airy' style of music coming into vogue in place of the older fantasias, and by 1680 only the bass viol remained in use.

Anthony Wood, in his reminiscences (*The Life and Times of Anthony Wood*, Andrew Clark (ed.), 1891) gives a detailed account of the various musical meetings that sprang up in Oxford during the Commonwealth. Music lovers gathered together once a week to listen to and play instrumental music. There were several regular clubs held in various college rooms, but the most important meeting was run by William Ellis at his home. Before the Commonwealth Ellis had been organist of St John's College, but now earned his living by arranging weekly meetings on a profit-making basis. As well as local musicians, Ellis invited visitors to Oxford to take part, such as the virtuoso violinist Thomas Baltzar (see Block 10, 'Restoration Music'). The step from this sort of meeting to the public concert was not far.

Wood was only interested in documenting the musical life of Oxford, although he does mention that an Oxford man, Edmund Chilmead, one of the chaplains of Christ Church Cathedral, moved to London during the Commonwealth and began a weekly musical meeting there. Henry Lawes also held a series of meetings, though rather select, at his house in London. It is possible that other clubs were started in London, and in other large towns around the country. Music could also be heard in taverns, despite the enactment of a further ordinance against vagrants, which included 'fiddlers or minstrels', in 1656–7. In and around London several taverns had music rooms or an area at one end of the room where the musicians sat, and entertainment was provided on request. It is perhaps rather ironical to note that some of the organs removed from churches found their way into taverns and were used there.

3 Music in the home

During the Commonwealth, consort music continued to be the most popular form of instrumental chamber music, and, following the death of William Lawes in 1645, John Jenkins (1592–1678) became the leading composer. His known output of instrumental compositions exceeds eight hundred items. His earlier works include many fantasias in four, five and six parts, in general of a more conservative nature than those of his contemporaries, but subsequently he 'became a reformer of music' (North (1846) *Memoirs of Music*, page 88). It is one of his later pieces that I want you to listen to now, the Fantasia from the First Suite for two trebles (violins) and two basses (viols). You can find it on record 1, side 2, band 4.

EXERCISE

How does this fantasia differ from the one you heard by William Lawes on record 1, side 1, band 6? (Lawes's fantasia is discussed in Block 2, pages 64–5. You will probably need to listen to the recording of Lawes's fantasia again.) Think in terms of the overall structure of the piece. For instance, you might say that Lawes's fantasia flows on in a long breath with no use of contrasting material to break the unity of the mood. Is this true of Jenkins's piece?

DISCUSSION

Jenkins's fantasia contains much more contrasting material in it than Lawes's. Although I suggested above that Lawes's fantasia uses no contrasting material, this is only true in the broadest terms. One could, for instance, suggest that it can be divided into three sections:

1, as far as the solo on bass viol;
2, as far as the sustained chord on all instruments; and
3, to the end.

1	2	3

The three different sections are based on different motives*. However, I think you'll agree that the different sections in the Jenkins fantasia are much more contrasted than those in the Lawes. Whereas the different sections in the Lawes do follow on from one another without much of a 'gear-change', those in Jenkins's piece are more discrete and individual in nature. This 'patchwork' effect is in fact typical of the later development of the fantasia.

EXERCISE

There are five sections in Jenkins's fantasia. Here's a list of these sections, with descriptions, but in the wrong order. Listen again to the piece right through, then fill in the missing numbers to indicate the correct order. Remember that between most sections there is no obvious break, the sections merge into one another. Also, the sections vary in length.

The opening: flowing, contrapuntal. [1]

A dance-like section, with a more straightforward rhythmic drive than the other sections. Chordal texture with tune at the top. [ ]

A slow section, partly chordal and partly contrapuntal, but with no obvious candidate for the tune. [ ]

Similar to the opening section, but much shorter and ending on a sustained chord. [ ]

A more florid section, full of quick, running notes. [ ]

DISCUSSION

1; 4; 3; 5; 2.

1	2	3	4	5
Contrapuntal flowing	Florid	Slow	Dance-like	Contrapuntal flowing

The type of material included in the fantasia has now become more varied. In contrast to the sort of texture we found in Lawes's earlier fantasia – as in sections 1, 3 and 5 – different types of writing are included: florid, almost virtuoso passages (section 2) and chordal, dance-like music (section 4). The homogeneous form of the earlier fantasia has developed into a more clearly sectional structure.

Although dance-like sections were introduced into the fantasia, separate dances, as in Lawes's Eighth Sonata, continued to be written, and the two remaining movements of Jenkins's Suite consist of an alman and corant*. Listen to the corant on record 1, side 2, band 5.

EXERCISE

How does the texture compare with the two dances from William Lawes's Eighth Sonata which you heard on record 1, side 1, bands 7 and 8? (see Block 2, page 65.)

DISCUSSION

The initial stages of a development away from contrapuntal writing to a more chordal texture that we saw in Lawes's alman and galliard is now taken a step further. The texture has polarized into a clear top and bottom part, with notes from the inner parts outlining the sequence of chords used in the piece. Sometimes, indeed, three of the four parts move forward together with the same rhythm, producing a series of chords. The top part is in fact shared by the two violins in a sort of dialogue. At the opening, for instance, the first violin plays a short motive, which is immediately imitated by the second violin. Then comes the first violin with another motive, which is again imitated by the second violin almost straightaway. This type of 'to-ing and fro-ing', a rudimentary type of counterpoint, was, as we shall see in Block 10, 'Restoration Music', typical of the later trio sonata*.

John Milton

Earlier in this discussion of Commonwealth music I noted that Milton was a dedicated music-lover. His father was in fact a composer and Milton was brought up to consider music a part of family life. He was later to write that 'soft Lydian airs' should be 'Married to immortal verse' ('L'Allegro'). In the next block we turn to a study of Milton and in reading his poetry it may help to remember his musical background.

Glossary

(The glossaries of musical terms are cumulative so you should refer back to Block 2 for terms which were first used there.)

Catch An English round (see below) of the seventeenth and eighteenth centuries, often humorous or bawdy in nature. Convivial drinking catches were the most numerous.

Corant A dance that originated in the sixteenth century and became a standard movement in the mid-seventeenth and eighteenth-century suite. Corant is an English corruption of the French 'courante'.

Dialogue A seventeenth-century vocal composition, usually for two parts with a question and answer text.

Lyra viol A viol which lies between the tenor and bass viols in size. The lyra viol was used particularly for solo playing.

Motive A short musical idea with a distinctive melodic and rhythmic shape.

Round A piece in which two or more voices sing an identical melody, each voice beginning at a different time (as in *Three Blind Mice*).

Trio sonata The most popular type of chamber music during the seventeenth century and first half of the eighteenth. Two upper parts shared a similar range and design and were supported by a bottom part.

Seventeenth-century England:
A Changing Culture, 1618–1689